Charcuterie Board Cookbook

150 mouthwatering recipes for learning how to pair cheeses, charcuterie, and mixed fruits. Turn the table into a stunning masterpiece with your family.

Contents

BUTTER BOARDS 5
- CRANBERRY & ALMOND BOARD .5
- ORANGE & WALNUTS BOARD 5
- FIGS & PISTACHIO BOARD 5
- CHERRIES & PISTACHIOS BOARD 5
- CRANBERRIES & PUMPKIN SEEDS BOARD 6
- MIXED NUTS BOARD 6
- POMEGRANATE & WALNUTs BOARD 6
- DRIED APPLE BOARD 6
- DRIED FRUIT BOARD 6
- ALMONDS BOARD 7
- NUTS & HERBS BOARD 7
- OLIVES & PINE NUTS BOARD 7
- OLIVES & RED PEPPER BOARD 8
- SUN-DRIED TOMATOES BOARD ... 8
- ONION & SAGE BOARD 8
- OLIVES BOARD 8
- TOMATO & WALNUT BOARD 8
- PROSCIUTTO BOARD 9
- BACON BOARD 9
- BELL PEPPER BOARD 9
- GREENS & SCALLION BOARD 10
- GREENS & WALNUTS BOARD 10
- ARTICHOKE & OLIVES BOARD ... 10
- PUMPKIN BUTTER BOARD 11
- CORN & COTTAGE CHEESE BOARD 11

BREAKFAST BOARDS 13
- FRUIT & MOZZARELLA BOARD .. 13
- BACON, EGGS & FRUIT BOARD ... 13
- PROSCIUTTO, EGGS & MOZZARELLA BOARD 13
- BACON, SALMON & EGGS BOARD 13
- SALMON, EGGS & VEGGIE BOARD 14
- HASH BROWN BOARD 14
- HASH BROWN & SCRAMBLED EGGS BOARD 15
- BISCUIT & SAUSAGE GRAVY BOARD 15
- VEGAN BISCUIT & GRAVY BOARD 16
- CREPES & BACON BOARD 16
- CREPES & FRUIT BOARD 17
- CREPES & TOFU SCRAMBLE BOARD 17
- PANCAKES, BACON & SAUSAGE BOARD 18
- PANCAKES, BACON & BERRIES BOARD 18
- PANCAKES, SAUSAGE & VEGGIE BOARD 19
- WAFFLES, BACON & SALMON BOARD 19
- WAFFLES & SCRAMBLED EGGS BOARD 20
- WAFFLES & BACON BOARD 20
- WAFFLES, FRUIT & ALMONDS BOARD 21
- WAFFLES, BACON & FRUIT BOARD 21
- BAGELS & FRUIT BOARD 22
- BAGELS, BACON & SALMON BOARD 22
- BAGELS & OATCAKE BISCUITS BOARD 22

- BAGEL & DELI MEAT BOARD 23
- FRENCH TOAST & BACON BOARD 23
- FRENCH TOAST & FRUIT BOARD 23
- FRENCH TOAST & NUTS BOARD 24
- FRENCH TOAST, BACON & SALMON BOARD 24
- FRENCH TOAST, HAM & SAUSAGE BOARD 25
- CROISSANT, HAM & SALAMI BOARD 25
- CROISSANT BOARD 25
- MUFFINS, FRUIT & ALONDS BOARD 26
- MUFFINS & CITRUS FRUIT BOARD 26
- MUFFINS & BERRIES BOARD 27
- MUFFINS, BACON & HASH BROWNS BOARD 27
- MUFFINS, KIELBASA & SALMON BOARD 28
- APPLE PORRIDGE BOARD 28
- QUINOA PORRIDGE BOARD 28
- OATS & FRUIT BOARD 29
- OATMEAL & MUFFINS BOARD 29

LUNCH, DINNER & SNACKS BOARDS 31

- ORANGE & OLIVES BOARD 31
- VEGGIES BOARD 31
- DELI MEAT, FRUIT & CHEESE BOARD 31
- SALMON & VEGGIES BOARD 32
- SALMON & FRUIT BOARD 32
- TABBOULEH & AVOCADO BOARD 32
- VEGGIES & YOGURT BOARD 33
- BEANS & POTATO BOARD 33
- TUNA & VEGGIES BOARD 34
- PEPPERONI & CHICKPEAS BOARD 34
- DELI MEAT & OLIVES BOARD 35
- DELI MEAT & BOCCONCINI BOARD 35
- DELI MEAT & FRUIT BOARD 35
- PICKLES & FRUIT BOARD 36
- DELI MEAT & ARTICHOKE BOARD 36
- SALAMI & PEPPERONI BOARD 37
- DELI PORK MEAT BOARD 37
- DELI MEAT & SALMON BOARD .. 38
- CALAMARI BOARD 38
- POTATO & OLIVES BOARD 39
- DELI MEAT & FOUR CHEESES BOARD 39
- VEGGIES & HUMMUS BOARD 40
- DELI MEAT & TROUT BOARD 40
- DELI MEAT & BERRIES BOARD .. 40
- CHICKEN SALAD BOARD 41
- SHRIMP SALAD BOARD 41
- POTATO SALAD BOARD 41
- CHICKEN SAUSAGE MEATBALLS BOARD 42
- PORK MEATBALLS BOARD 42
- LAMB MEATBALLS BOARD 43
- BEEF MEATBALLS BOARD 43
- TURKEY MEATBALLS BOARD 43
- VEGGIE LOAF BOARD 44
- BEEF MEATLOAF BOARD 44
- LEMONY CHICKEN WINGS BOARD 45

BUFFALO CHICKEN WINGS BOARD 45	DIPPING SAUCES RECIPES 57
LAMB CHOPS BOARD 46	YOGURT TZATZIKI 57
LAMB CHOPS BOARD 46	LEMONY FETA SAUCE 57
SHRIMP BOARD 47	WARM CHEESE SAUCE 57
CRISPY SHRIMP BOARD 47	LEMONY GARLIC SAUCE 57
FISH STICKS BOARD 48	WALNUT & BREAD SAUCE 58
ONION RINGS & FRIES BOARD ... 48	BEET HUMMUS 58
BEEF BURGERS BOARD 49	CARROT HUMMUS 58
VEGETARIAN BURGERS BOARD . 49	CHICKPEAS HUMMUS 58
GAZPACHO BOARD 50	WHITE BEANS SAUCE 59
SWEET POTATO SOUP BOARD 50	BABA GHANOUSH 59
TOMATO SOUP BOARD 50	PESTO SAUCE 59
CARROT SOUP BOARD 51	HERB SAUCE 60
FRENCH ONION SOUP BOARD ... 52	NUTTY ROMESCO SAUCE 60
DESSERT BOARD RECIPES 53	CHEESY RED PEPPER SAUCE 60
ICE CREAM & FRUIT BOARD 53	POMEGRANATE BBQ SAUCE 61
YOGURT & FRUIT BOARD 53	FRUITY BBQ SAUCE 61
CANDIES & FRUIT BOARD 53	MANGO SAUCE 61
COOKIES & NUTS BOARD 54	FRUITY SAUCE 62
COOKIES & JELLY BEANS BOARD 54	PEANUT BUTTER SAUCE 62
COOKIES & FRUIT BOARD 54	HONEY MUSTARD 62
POPCORN & TRUFFLES BOARD .. 54	HONEY CREAM SAUCE 62
PRATZELS & COOKIES BOARD 55	CREAMY MARSHMALLOW SAUCE 62
PRETZELS & CANDIES BOARD ... 55	CARAMEL SAUCE 62
CHOCOLATE PRETZELS & WAFERS BOARD 55	CHOCOLATE SAUCE 63
CHOCOLATE & DRIED FRUIT BOARD 55	HOT FUDGE SAUCE 63
	SHOPPING LIST 64
	INDEX 68

BUTTER BOARDS

CRANBERRY & ALMOND BOARD
Prep Time: 10 mins. | Serves: 8

- 1 C. unsalted butter, softened
- ¼ C. dried cranberries
- ¼ C. almonds, sliced
- 2 tbsp. candied ginger, chopped
- 1 tbsp. fresh rosemary, finely chopped
- 1½ tsp. lemon zest, grated
- 2 tbsp. honey
- 16 crusty bread slices, toasted

1. Place the butter in a medium-sized glass bowl and with a silicone spatula, stir until smooth.
2. Spread the butter onto a serving wooden board and top with cranberries, almonds, ginger, rosemary and lemon zest.
3. Drizzle with honey and serve alongside the bread slices.

Per Serving:
Calories: 358 | Fat: 25.6g | Carbs: 28.8g | Fiber: 1.7g | Protein: 4.4g

ORANGE & WALNUTS BOARD
Prep Time: 10 mins. | Serves: 8

- 1 C. unsalted butter, softened
- 1 tbsp. brown sugar
- 1/8 tsp. ground cinnamon
- 1/8 tsp. ground nutmeg
- Pinch of ground ginger
- 3 candied oranges
- 2 tbsp. walnuts, chopped
- 16 Brioche bread slices, toasted

1. Place the butter in a medium-sized glass bowl and with a silicone spatula, stir until smooth.
2. Spread the butter onto a serving wooden board evenly.
3. Sprinkle the top of butter with brown sugar and spices.
4. Top with oranges and walnuts and serve alongside the bread slices.

Per Serving:
Calories: 520 | Fat: 28.7g | Carbs: 62.9g | Fiber: 0.2g | Protein: 4.7g

FIGS & PISTACHIO BOARD
Prep Time: 15 mins. | Serves: 10

- 12 oz. salted butter, softened
- 1 tbsp. roasted garlic, lightly smashed
- 1 tbsp. fresh herbs (parsley, basil, rosemary, thyme, chives), finely chopped
- ½ tsp. flaky salt
- ¼ tsp. ground black pepper
- 1 tsp. lemon zest, grated
- 1 tbsp. Parmesan cheese, grated
- 3-4 fresh basil leaves, shredded
- 4 fresh figs, thinly sliced
- ¼-1/3 C. honey
- 4 tbsp. pistachios
- 2 fresh mint leaves, sliced thinly
- 20 crusty bread slices, toasted

1. Place the butter and garlic in a medium-sized glass bowl and with a silicone spatula, stir until smooth.
2. Spread the butter onto a serving wooden board and sprinkle with herbs, salt and black pepper.
3. Drizzle with honey and top with remaining ingredients.
4. Top with red peppers and olives and drizzle with basil oil.
5. Serve alongside the bread slices.

Per Serving:
Calories: 417 | Fat: 29.5g | Carbs: 35.7g | Fiber: 2g | Protein: 4.7g

CHERRIES & PISTACHIOS BOARD
Prep Time: 10 mins. | Serves: 8

- 1 C. unsalted butter, softened
- 1 tsp. flaky salt
- 3 tbsp. fig jam
- 1 tbsp. honey
- 2 tbsp. pistachios
- 2 tbsp. dried cherries
- 2 boxes fig and olive crisps

1. Place the butter in a medium-sized glass bowl and with a silicone spatula, stir until smooth.
2. Spread the butter onto a serving wooden board evenly and then sprinkle it with salt.
3. Top with jam, honey, pistachios and cherries and serve alongside the crisps.

Per Serving:
Calories: 385 | Fat: 23.5g | Carbs: 43g | Fiber: 2g | Protein: 1.9g

CRANBERRIES & PUMPKIN SEEDS BOARD

Prep Time: 10 mins. | Serves: 8

- 1 C. unsalted butter, softened
- ¼ tsp. salt
- 2 tbsp. dried cranberries, chopped
- 2 tbsp. pumpkin seeds
- 1 tbsp. walnuts, chopped
- 2 tbsp. fresh basil, chopped
- 2 tsp. fresh chives, chopped
- Dash of fresh lemon juice
- 16 French bread slices, toasted

1. Place the butter in a medium-sized glass bowl and with a silicone spatula, stir until smooth.
2. Spread the butter onto a serving wooden board evenly and then sprinkle it with salt.
3. Top with cranberries, pumpkin seeds, walnuts, basil and chives.
4. Drizzle with lemon juice and serve alongside the bread slices

Per Serving:
Calories: 330 | Fat: 24.5g | Carbs: 23.3g | Fiber: 1.4g | Protein: 5.8g

MIXED NUTS BOARD

Prep Time: 15 mins. | Cook Time: 5 mins. | Serves: 12

- 1/3 C. walnuts, roughly chopped
- 1/3 C. pistachios, roughly chopped
- 1 lb. unsalted butter, softened
- 3 tbsp. honey
- ½ tsp. ground cinnamon
- Flaky salt, as needed
- 24 ciabatta bread slices, toasted

1. Preheat your oven to 350 °F.
2. Place the walnuts and pistachios onto a cookie sheet and then arrange in a single layer.
3. Bake for approximately 4-5 minutes.
4. Remove the cookie sheet of walnuts and pistachios from oven and set it aside to cool.
5. Place the butter in a medium-sized glass bowl and with a silicone spatula, stir until smooth.
6. Spread the butter onto a serving wooden board and drizzle with honey.
7. Top with roasted nuts and sprinkle with cinnamon and salt.
8. Serve alongside the bread slices.

Per Serving:
Calories: 451 | Fat: 35.1g | Carbs: 30.5g | Fiber: 1.7g | Protein: 5.3g

POMEGRANATE & WALNUTs BOARD

Prep Time: 10 mins. | Serves: 8

- 1 C. unsalted butter, softened
- ¼ C. strawberry jam
- ¼ C. honey
- ¼ tsp. ground cinnamon
- ¼ C. pomegranate seeds
- ¼ C. walnuts, chopped
- 1 tsp. lemon zest, grated
- 16 crusty bread slices, toasted

1. Place the butter in a medium-sized glass bowl and with a silicone spatula, stir until smooth.
2. Spread the butter onto a serving wooden board and top with jam in the shape of dollops.
3. Drizzle with honey and sprinkle with cinnamon.
4. Top with pomegranate seeds, walnuts and lemon zest and serve alongside the bread slices.

Per Serving:
Calories: 488 | Fat: 34.9g | Carbs: 40.3g | Fiber: 0.4g | Protein: 5.4g

DRIED APPLE BOARD

Prep Time: 15 mins. | Serves: 8

- 1 C. unsalted butter, softened
- 2 tbsp. fresh thyme, chopped
- ¼ C. honey
- ¼ C. microgreens
- ¼ C. dried apples
- ¼ tsp. sea salt
- 16 baguette bread slices, toasted

1. Place the butter and thyme in a medium-sized glass bowl and with a silicone spatula, stir until smooth.
2. Spread the butter onto a serving wooden board and drizzle with honey.
3. Top with greens and dried apples and sprinkle with salt.
4. Serve alongside the bread slices.

Per Serving:
Calories: 398 | Fat: 30.5g | Carbs: 26.9g | Fiber: 1g | Protein: 4.9g

DRIED FRUIT BOARD

Prep Time: 10 mins. | Serves: 8

- 8 oz. unsalted butter, softened
- 2 tbsp. honey
- 1 tsp. lemon zest, grated
- 2 tbsp. dried strawberries

- 2 tbsp. dried tangerines
- 2 tbsp. dried peaches
- ¼ tsp. sea salt
- 2 tsp. fresh rosemary, minced
- 16 crostini bread slices, toasted

1. Place the butter in a medium-sized glass bowl and with a silicone spatula, stir until smooth.
2. Spread the butter onto a serving wooden board and drizzle with honey.
3. Top with lemon zest and dried fruit.
4. Sprinkle with salt and rosemary and serve alongside the bread slices.

Per Serving:
Calories: 370| Fat: 24.8g| Carbs: 33.9g| Fiber: 2g| Protein: 4.5g

ALMONDS BOARD
Prep Time: 10 mins.| Serves: 8

- 1 C. unsalted butter, softened
- ¼ C. apricot jam
- 4 tbsp. almonds, chopped
- 1 tbsp. orange zest, grated
- 1 tsp. fresh rosemary leaves, chopped
- ¼ tsp. red chili flakes
- 16 sourdough bread slices, toasted

1. Place the butter in a medium-sized glass bowl and with a silicone spatula, stir until smooth.
2. Spread the butter onto a serving wooden board and spoon the apricot jam on top in the shape of dots.
3. Top with almonds, orange zest and rosemary and sprinkle with chili flakes.
4. Serve alongside the bread slices.

Per Serving:
Calories: 380| Fat: 25.8g| Carbs: 33g| Fiber: 1.8g| Protein: 5.8g

NUTS & HERBS BOARD
Prep Time: 15 mins.| Cook Time: 1 min.| Serves: 8

- 4 tbsp. olive oil
- 3 garlic cloves, thinly sliced
- 1 C. unsalted butter, softened
- ½ C. mixed nuts, crushed
- 1 tbsp. fresh dill, chopped
- 1 tbsp. fresh chives, thinly sliced
- 2 tsp. orange zest, grated
- 1 tsp. lemon zest, grated
- 1 tbsp. sea salt
- 1 tsp. red pepper flakes, crushed
- 3 tbsp. honey
- 16 Baguette bread slices, toasted

1. Heat oil in a small-sized, heavy-bottomed wok over a medium heat and cook garlic slices for approximately 30 seconds per side.
2. Remove the garlic slices from wok and place them onto a paper towel-lined dish.
3. Place the butter in a medium-sized glass bowl and with a silicone spatula, stir until smooth.
4. Spread the butter onto a serving wooden board and top with nuts, herbs, garlic slices and zest.
5. Sprinkle the top of butter with salt and red pepper flakes and then drizzle it with honey.
6. Serve alongside the bread.

Per Serving:
Calories: 491| Fat: 36.1g| Carbs: 37.7g| Fiber: 1.9g| Protein: 7.8g

OLIVES & PINE NUTS BOARD
Prep Time: 15 mins.| Cook Time: 35 mins.| Serves: 12

- 2 small garlic heads
- 1 tsp. olive oil
- Sea salt and ground black pepper, as needed
- 1 lb. unsalted butter, unsalted
- 1/3 C. green olives, pitted and sliced
- 1/3 C. kalamata olives, pitted and sliced
- 4 tbsp. pine nuts, toasted
- ½ tsp. Za'atar
- 24 crusty bread slices, toasted

1. Preheat your oven to 400 °F.
2. With a small-sized knife, remove the top of both garlic heads.
3. Lightly coat the garlic heads with oil evenly.
4. Then sprinkle them with salt and pepper.
5. With a piece of heavy-duty foil, wrap the garlic heads.
6. Place the foil packet of garlic onto a rimmed cookie sheet.
7. Bake for approximately 32-35 minutes.
8. Remove the cookie sheet of wrapped garlic heads from oven and place onto a counter.
9. Unwrap the garlic heads and set them aside to cool.
10. Squeeze the garlic heads into a medium-sized glass bowl.
11. In the bowl of roasted garlic, place the butter and mix until finely blended.
12. Spread the butter onto a serving wooden board and top with olives and pine nuts.
13. Sprinkle with Za'atar and serve alongside the bread slices.

Per Serving:

Calories: 494| Fat: 43.5g| Carbs: 22.7g| Fiber: 0.4g| Protein: 5.1g

OLIVES & RED PEPPER BOARD
Prep Time: 10 mins.| Serves: 8

- ½ lb. unsalted butter, softened
- 2 garlic cloves, finely minced
- 2 tsp. olive oil
- 2 tsp. fresh basil, minced
- ½ tsp. flaky salt
- ¼ C. jarred roasted red peppers, chopped
- ¼ C. green olives, pitted and sliced
- 16 baguette bread slices, toasted, toasted

1. Place the butter and garlic in a medium-sized glass bowl and with a silicone spatula, stir until smooth.
2. In a small-sized bowl, blend together the minced basil and oil.
3. Spread the butter onto a serving wooden board evenly and then sprinkle it with salt.
4. Top with red peppers and olives and drizzle with basil oil.
5. Serve alongside the bread slices.

Per Serving:
Calories: 354| Fat: 26.3g| Carbs: 26.2g| Fiber: 1.4g| Protein: 4.2g

SUN-DRIED TOMATOES BOARD
Prep Time: 15 mins.| Serves: 8

- 1 C. unsalted butter, softened
- 2 garlic cloves, finely minced
- ½ C. sun-dried tomatoes, drained and chopped
- 2 tbsp. fresh basil leaves, shredded
- 2 tbsp. Parmesan cheese, grated
- 1 tbsp. pine nuts
- Pinch of flaky salt
- 1 tbsp. balsamic vinaigrette
- 16 crusty bread slices, toasted

1. Place the butter and garlic in a medium-sized glass bowl and with a silicone spatula, stir until smooth.
2. Spread the butter onto a serving wooden board and top with tomatoes, basil, Parmesan cheese and pine nuts
3. Sprinkle with salt and drizzle with balsamic vinaigrette.
4. Serve alongside the bread slices.

Per Serving:
Calories: 526| Fat: 27.8g| Carbs: 61g| Fiber: 2.2g| Protein: 9.1g

ONION & SAGE BOARD
Prep Time: 10 mins.| Serves: 8

- 1 C. unsalted butter, softened
- Pinch of flaky salt
- 1 tsp. ground black pepper
- 6 roasted garlic cloves, mashed
- 1 tsp. lemon zest, grated
- ½ of small red onion, sliced
- 1 tsp. fresh sage, chopped
- 1 tsp. maple syrup
- 16 baguette bread slices, toasted

1. Place the butter in a medium-sized glass bowl and with a silicone spatula, stir until smooth.
2. Spread the butter onto a serving wooden board evenly and then sprinkle it with salt and black pepper.
3. Top with garlic, lemon zest, onion and sage
4. Drizzle with maple syrup and serve alongside the bread slices.

Per Serving:
Calories: 368| Fat: 30.5g| Carbs: 18.5g| Fiber: 0.8g| Protein: 5g

OLIVES BOARD
Prep Time: 10 mins.| Serves: 8

- 1 C. salted butter, softened
- 2 tbsp. hot honey
- 1/3 C. marinated olives, chopped
- 1 tbsp. fresh parsley, finely chopped
- 16 baguette bread slices, toasted

1. Place the butter in a medium-sized glass bowl and with a silicone spatula, stir until smooth.
2. Spread the butter onto a serving wooden board and drizzle with oney.
3. Top with olives and parsley and serve alongside the bread slices.

Per Serving:
Calories: 382| Fat: 31.1g| Carbs: 21.2g| Fiber: 0.7g| Protein: 4.8g

TOMATO & WALNUT BOARD
Prep Time: 15 mins.| Cook Time: 15 mins.| Serves: 8

- 2 C. cherry tomatoes
- 2 tbsp. olive oil
- Salt and ground black pepper, as needed
- ½ C. liquid honey
- ½ tsp. red chili flakes

- ¼ tsp. Dijon mustard
- 1 C. salted butter, softened
- 2 jalapeño peppers, sliced thinly
- ½ C. walnuts, chopped
- 16 baguette bread slices, toasted, toasted

1. Preheat your oven to 425 °F.
2. Line a small-sized, rimmed cookie sheet with baking paper.
3. Place the cherry tomatoes onto the prepared cookie sheet.
4. Drizzle the tomatoes with oil evenly.
5. Sprinkle with salt and black pepper and then arrange in a single layer.
6. Bake for approximately 15 minutes.
7. Remove the cookie sheet of baked tomatoes from oven and let them cool completely.
8. Blend together the mustard, honey and chili flakes in a small-sized bowl.
9. Place the butter in a medium-sized glass bowl and with a silicone spatula, stir until smooth.
10. Spread the butter onto a serving wooden board and top with tomatoes.
11. Drizzle with honey mixture and sprinkle with a pinch of salt.
12. Top with jalapeño peppers and walnuts and serve alongside the bread slices.

Per Serving:
Calories: 512| Fat: 38.8g| Carbs: 36.8g| Fiber: 1.8g| Protein: 7.1g

PROSCIUTTO BOARD

Prep Time: 20 mins.| Cook Time: 10 mins.| Serves: 8

- 6 oz. salted butter, softened
- 1½ tbsp. olive oil
- 2 shallots, finely chopped
- 1 tsp. red chilli flakes
- 1 lemon
- Flaky salt, as needed
- 3 oz. prosciutto slices
- 1 tsp. fresh parsley, chopped
- 16 crusty bread slices, toasted, toasted

1. Heat a medium-sized, heavy-bottomed wok over a medium-high heat and cook the prosciutto slices for approximately 8-10 minutes.
2. Remove the prosciutto slices from wok and place them onto a paper towel-lined dish.
3. Meanwhile, heat oil in a small-sized, non-stick frying pan over a medium heat and cook the shallots, chilli flakes and a pinch of salt for approximately 8-10 minutes or until caramelised, stirring frequently.
4. Remove the frying pan of shallot from heat and set aside.
5. Chop the prosciutto slices into small-sized pieces.
6. Place the butter in a medium-sized glass bowl and with a silicone spatula, stir until smooth.
7. Spread the butter onto a serving wooden board and top with caramelised shallot mix and lemon zest.
8. Top with prosciutto and parsley and serve alongside the bread slices.

Per Serving:
Calories: 311| Fat: 21.5g| Carbs: 24.2g| Fiber: 1.1g| Protein: 6.1g

BACON BOARD

Prep Time: 15 mins.| Cook Time: 10 mins.| Serves: 8

- 4 thick-cut bacon slices
- 8 oz. unsalted butter, softened
- 3 tbsp. maple syrup, divided
- ½ tsp. salt
- 1 tbsp. scallion greens, chopped
- 16 cinnamon bread slices, toasted, toasted

1. Heat a heavy-bottomed wok over a medium-high heat and cook the bacon for approximately 8-10 minutes, flipping periodically.
2. Remove the cooked bacon from wok and place onto a paper towel-lined dish.
3. Set it aside to cool.
4. Chop 2 bacon slices finely.
5. Then chop remaining butter slices roughly.
6. In a medium-sized glass bowl, add the softened butter, 2 tbsp. of maple syrup and salt and whisk until blended and smooth.
7. Add the finely chopped bacon slices and stir to blend.
8. Spread the butter onto a serving wooden board and drizzle with maple syrup.
9. Top with remaining chopped bacon and scallion greens.
10. Serve alongside the bread slices.

Per Serving:
Calories: 447| Fat: 31.7g| Carbs: 29.1g| Fiber: 2.7g| Protein: 9.6g

BELL PEPPER BOARD

Prep Time: 15 mins.| Serves: 8

- 1 C. salted butter, softened
- 1 tsp. garlic, grated
- 1 tsp. red chili flakes
- Pinch of flaky salt

- ½ C. onion, finely chopped
- ¾ C. bell peppers, seeded and finely chopped
- 2 tbsp. scallion greens, finely chopped
- ¼ C. cottage cheese, grated
- 1 tsp. honey
- 3 C. oyster crackers

1. Place the butter in a medium-sized glass bowl and with a silicone spatula, stir until smooth.
2. Spread the butter onto a serving wooden board and sprinkle with garlic, chili flakes and salt.
3. Top with onion, bell peppers, scallion greens and cottage cheese.
4. Drizzle with honey and serve alongside the crackers.

Per Serving:
Calories: 337| Fat: 29.1g| Carbs: 16.9g| Fiber: 0.7g| Protein: 3.2g

GREENS & SCALLION BOARD
Prep Time: 15 mins.| Cook Time: 40 mins.| Serves: 8

- 1 whole garlic head
- ½ tbsp. olive oil
- Salt and ground black pepper, as needed
- 1 C. unsalted butter, softened
- 2 tsp. honey
- Flaky salt, as needed
- 1 tsp. red pepper flakes, crushed
- 1 tsp. lemon zest, grated
- ¼ tsp. dried thyme
- ¼ tsp. dried basil
- ½ C. microgreens
- 2 tbsp. scallion greens, chopped
- 16 crusty French bread slices, toasted, toasted

1. Preheat your oven to 400 °F.
2. Cut off the top of garlic head.
3. Lightly coat the garlic head with olive oil evenly and then sprinkle it with salt and black pepper.
4. With a piece of heavy-duty foil, wrap the oiled garlic head.
5. Place the foil packet of garlic onto a small-sized, rimmed cookie sheet.
6. Bake for approximately 32-40 minutes.
7. Remove the cookie sheet of wrapped garlic head from oven and place onto a counter.
8. Unwrap the garlic head and set it aside to cool.
9. Squeeze the garlic head into a medium-sized glass bowl.
10. In the bowl of roasted garlic, add the butter and mix until finely blended.
11. Spread the butter onto a serving wooden board and drizzle with honey.
12. Sprinkle with salt, red pepper flakes, lemon zest and dried herbs.
13. Top with greens and scallion greens and serve alongside the bread slices.

Per Serving:
Calories: 370| Fat: 24.9g| Carbs: 31.7g| Fiber: 1.5g| Protein: 6.6g

GREENS & WALNUTS BOARD
Prep Time: 15 mins.| Serves: 8

- 1 C. unsalted butter, softened
- ½ C. fresh mixed herbs, finely chopped
- 1 tsp. fine grain salt
- 1 C. fresh baby greens
- 4 tbsp. walnuts, chopped
- 1 tsp. lemon zest, grated
- 16 French bread slices, toasted

1. Place the butter, herbs and salt in a medium-sized glass bowl and with a silicone spatula, stir until smooth.
2. Spread the butter onto a serving wooden board and top with greens, walnuts and lemon zest.
3. Serve alongside the bread slices.

Per Serving:
Calories: 367| Fat: 26.5g| Carbs: 27.4g| Fiber: 2.3g| Protein: 6g

ARTICHOKE & OLIVES BOARD
Prep Time: 15 mins.| Serves: 8

- 1 C. unsalted butter, softened
- 3 garlic cloves, minced
- 1 tsp. lemon zest, grated
- 1 tsp. fresh oregano, minced
- 1 tsp. fresh thyme, minced
- ½ tsp. sea salt
- Splash of champagne
- ½ C. olives, pitted
- ½ C. marinated artichoke heart, chopped
- 16 crusty bread slices, toasted

1. Place the butter in a medium-sized glass bowl and with a silicone spatula, stir until smooth.
2. Spread the butter onto a serving wooden board and top with garlic, lemon zest, fresh herbs and salt.
3. Drizzle with champagne and top with olives and artichoke.
4. Serve alongside the bread slices.

Per Serving:

Calories: 334| Fat: 25g| Carbs: 24.6g| Fiber: 1.6g| Protein: 4.1g

PUMPKIN BUTTER BOARD

Prep Time: 20 mins.| **Cook Time:** 10 mins.| **Serves:** 10

For Pumpkin Butter
- 1 C. canned pumpkin puree
- ¼ C. maple syrup
- 1-2 tsp. pumpkin pie spice
- 1/8 tsp. sea salt
- 1 C. unsalted butter, softened

For Crispy Sage
- 2 tbsp. unsalted butter
- 1 bunch fresh sage leaves

For Board
- 3 tbsp. maple syrup
- 1 tsp. pumpkin pie spice
- 2 tbsp. pumpkin seeds, toasted
- 2 tbsp. dried cranberries
- 2 tbsp. pecans
- ½ tsp. flaky salt
- 16 crusty bread slices, toasted

1. For pumpkin butter: add the pumpkin puree, maple syrup, pumpkin pie spice and salt in a small-sized, heavy-bottomed saucepan and mix thoroughly.
2. Place the pan of pumpkin puree mixture over a medium-low heat and cook for 7 minutes, stirring continually.
3. Remove the pan of pumpkin puree mixture from heat and transfer it into a heat-proof glass bowl.
4. Set it aside to cool completely.
5. Place the butter in a medium-sized glass bowl and with a silicone spatula, stir until smooth.
6. Add the pumpkin puree mixture and stir until smooth. Set aside.
7. For crispy sage leaves; melt the butter in a small-sized saucepan over a medium heat and cook the sage leaves for approximately 2 minutes, stirring continually.
8. Remove the sage leaves from saucepan and place them onto a paper towel-lined dish to cool.
9. Spread the pumpkin butter onto a serving wooden board and top with crispy sage leaves.
10. Drizzle with maple syrup and sprinkle with pumpkin spice, pumpkin seeds, salt, cranberries, and pecans.
11. Serve alongside the bread slices.

Per Serving:

Calories: 297| Fat: 19.7g| Carbs: 27.7g| Fiber: 1.7g| Protein: 3.6g

CORN & COTTAGE CHEESE BOARD

Prep Time: 25 mins.| **Cook Time:** 8 mins.| **Serves:** 8

For Corn & Cheese
- 2 tbsp. plain Greek yogurt
- 1 tbsp. plus 2 tsp. canola oil, divided
- 1 tsp. fresh lemon juice
- 2 tsp. chickpeas flour, roasted
- ½ tsp. dried fenugreek leaves
- ½ tsp. red chili powder
- ½ tsp. ground coriander
- ¼ tsp. ground turmeric
- ¼ tsp. garam masala powder
- Salt, as needed
- ½ C. frozen corn
- ½ C. cottage cheese, cut into small cubes
- ½ tsp. ginger paste
- ½ tsp. garlic paste

For Board
- 6 oz. unsalted butter, softened
- 2 tbsp. bell pepper, seeded and finely chopped
- 2 tbsp. red onion, finely chopped
- 1 tbsp. fresh cilantro, finely chopped
- ¼ C. mango chutney
- 16 crusty bread slices, toasted

1. For marinade: in a large-sized bowl, add yogurt, 2 tsp. of canola oil, lemon juice, chickpeas flour, spices and salt and mix until finely blended.
2. Add the corn and cheese cubes and coat with marinade generously.
3. Refrigerate for at least 2 hours.
4. Heat remaining canola oil in a large-sized heavy-bottomed wok over a medium heat and cook the corn and cheese cubes for approximately 5-6 minutes, stirring frequently.
5. Add in the garlic and ginger paste and cook for 1-2 minutes, stirring continually.
6. Remove the wok of corn mixture from heat and let it cool.
7. Place the butter in a medium-sized glass bowl and with a silicone spatula, stir until smooth.
8. Spread the butter onto a serving wooden board and top with corn mixture, bell pepper, onion and cilantro.
9. Drizzle with mango chutney and serve alongside the bread slices.

Per Serving:
Calories: 343| Fat: 21.5g| Carbs: 32.3g| Fiber: 1.9g| Protein: 6.7g

BREAKFAST BOARDS

FRUIT & MOZZARELLA BOARD
Prep Time: 15 mins. | Serves: 8

- 8 oz. container fresh mozzarella cheese salad pearls
- 8 oz. container marinated fresh mozzarella cheese balls
- 3 oz. prosciutto
- 4 oz. salami
- 2 oz. Kalamata olives
- 4 C. cherry tomatoes
- 2 ripe peaches, pitted and sliced
- ½ of medium cantaloupe, peeled and cubed
- 1 baguette bread, cut into cubes
- 4 C. fresh baby arugula
- 3 oz. almonds, roasted
- ¼ C. balsamic glaze

1. Arrange a large-sized serving platter in the middle of a wooden board. Set aside.
2. Arrange all ingredients except for balsamic glaze onto the platter over the board.
3. Drizzle with balsamic glaze and serve immediately.

Per Serving:
Calories: 410 | Fat: 20.8g | Carbs: 30.9g | Fiber: 4.3g | Protein: 27.6g

BACON, EGGS & FRUIT BOARD
Prep Time: 15 mins. | Cook Time: 20 mins. | Serves: 6

- 12 bacon slices
- 6 baguette bread slices, toasted
- 6 hard-boiled eggs, peeled and halved
- 6 tbsp. unsalted butter
- 6 tbsp. strawberry jam
- 12 fresh strawberries
- 3 bananas, peeled and sliced
- 1½ C. cherry tomatoes, halved
- 1 large avocado, peeled, pitted and sliced
- Flaked sea salt, as needed

1. Preheat your oven to 400 °F.
2. Line a large-sized cookie sheet with baking paper.
3. Place the bacon slices onto the prepared cookie sheet and then arrange them in a single leer.
4. Bake for approximately 19-20 minutes.
5. Meanwhile, arrange the bread slices onto a second cookie sheet.
6. Transfer the cookie sheet of bread slices into the oven and bake for approximately 9-10 minutes, flipping once halfway through.
7. Remove both cookie sheets from oven.
8. With tongs, place the cooked bacon slices onto a paper towel-lined dish.
9. Arrange a large-sized serving platter in the middle of a wooden board. Set aside.
10. In 2 small-sized bowls, place the butter and jam respectively.
11. Arrange the bowls of butter and jam onto the platter over the board.
12. Then, arrange the bread slices, bacon slices and remaining ingredients onto the platter around the bowls.
13. Sprinkle with salt and serve immediately.

Per Serving:
Calories: 745 | Fat: 50.8g | Carbs: 42.4g | Fiber: 5g | Protein: 31.3g

PROSCIUTTO, EGGS & MOZZARELLA BOARD
Prep Time: 15 mins. | Serves: 8

- ½ C. strawberry jam
- ½ C. unsalted butter, softened
- 16 prosciutto slices
- 8 sourdough bread slices, toasted, toasted
- 8 soft-boiled eggs, peeled and halved
- 1½ C. mozzarella cheese balls
- 1 cantaloupe, peeled and cut into wedges
- ½ C. fresh blueberries
- 2 large avocados, halved, pitted, peeled, and sliced
- 2 large tomatoes, sliced

1. Arrange a large-sized serving platter in the middle of a wooden board. Set aside.
2. In 2 small-sized bowls, place the jam and butter respectively.
3. Arrange the bowls of jam and butter onto the platter over the board.
4. Arrange the remaining ingredients onto the platter around the bowls and serve.

Per Serving:
Calories: 480 | Fat: 31g | Carbs: 33.7g | Fiber: 4.9g | Protein: 20.3g

BACON, SALMON & EGGS BOARD
Prep Time: 20 mins. | Serves: 8

- ✓ 1 banana, peeled and cut into ½-inch thick slices
- ✓ 2 tbsp. fresh lemon juice
- ✓ 2-3 large, ripe avocados, peeled and pitted
- ✓ 1 tbsp. red chili flakes
- ✓ 8 whole-wheat bread slices, toasted, toasted
- ✓ 1 C. fresh yellow corn
- ✓ 1 C. red salsa
- ✓ ½ C. pesto
- ✓ ¼ C. honey
- ✓ 8 cooked bacon slices
- ✓ 8 oz. smoked salmon
- ✓ 8 soft-boiled eggs, peeled and halved
- ✓ 2 large tomatoes, sliced
- ✓ ½ C. Cotija cheese, crumbled
- ✓ ½ C. goat cheese, crumbled
- ✓ 4 oz. fresh microgreens
- ✓ 4 oranges, peeled, seeded and sliced
- ✓ ½ C. coconut flakes

1. Arrange a large-sized serving platter in the middle of a wooden board. Set aside.
2. Place the banana slices in a glass bowl and drizzle them with lemon juice lightly.
3. In a separate owl, place the avocado slices, red chili flakes and some lemon juice
4. With a fork, mash the avocado slices.
5. Spread the mashed avocado onto each bread slice evenly.
6. In 4 small-sized bowls, place the corn, salsa, pesto and honey.
7. Arrange the bowls of corn, salsa, pesto and honey onto the platter over the board.
8. Arrange the bread slices, banana slices and remaining ingredients onto the platter around the bowls and serve.

Per Serving:
Calories: 649| Fat: 39.6g| Carbs: 48.7g| Fiber: 10.5g| Protein: 32g

SALMON, EGGS & VEGGIE BOARD
Prep Time: 15 mins.| Serves: 6

- ✓ 6 tbsp. raspberry jelly
- ✓ 6 tbsp. unsalted butter, softened
- ✓ 6 hard-boiled eggs, peeled and halved lengthwise
- ✓ 6 oz. smoked salmon
- ✓ 1 large avocado, peeled, pitted and sliced
- ✓ ½ of red onion, sliced
- ✓ 3 radishes, sliced
- ✓ 1 English cucumber, sliced
- ✓ 1½ C. cherry tomatoes
- ✓ 2-3 tbsp. everything bagel seasoning

1. Arrange a large-sized serving platter in the middle of a wooden board. Set aside.
2. In 2 small-sized bowls, place the raspberry jelly and butter respectively.
3. Arrange the bowls of jelly and butter onto the platter over the board.
4. Arrange the eggs, salmon, avocado, and veggie around the bowls.
5. Sprinkle with bagel seasoning and serve.

Per Serving:
Calories: 352| Fat: 23.8g| Carbs: 23.5g| Fiber: 3.5g| Protein: 12.4g

HASH BROWN BOARD
Prep Time: 20 mins.| Cook Time: 24 mins.| Serves: 8

For Hash Browns
- ✓ 2 lb. Russet potatoes, scrubbed and grated
- ✓ ½ tsp. garlic powder
- ✓ ½ tsp. onion powder
- ✓ Salt, as needed
- ✓ ½ C. olive oil

For Board
- ✓ 1 C. sour cream
- ✓ 1 C. fig jam
- ✓ 8 poached eggs
- ✓ 8 cooked bacon slices
- ✓ 8 oz. salami
- ✓ 8 oz. smoked salmon
- ✓ 1 C. olives, pitted
- ✓ 3 C. fresh baby arugula

1. For hash browns: place the grated potatoes in a fine-mesh sieve and rinse them under cold water thoroughly.
2. Drain the potatoes well.
3. Through a clean tea towel, remove the moisture from the potatoes completely.
4. Transfer potato into a bowl with garlic powder, onion powder and salt and mix until finely blended.
5. Heat ¼ C. of oil in a large-sized cast-iron wok over a medium heat and place half of the potatoes.
6. In the wok, spread the potatoes in an even layer and then with the back of spoon, press them down.
7. Cook for 1½-2 minutes without stirring.
8. Stir the potatoes gently and again, press them down.
9. Cook for 1½-2 minutes.
10. Cook for 7-8 minutes, stirring and pressing after every 2 minutes.
11. Meanwhile, line a late-sized plate with a 2-3 layers of paper towels.

12. Transfer the hash browns onto paper towels-lined plate to drain.
13. Repeat with the remaining oil and potatoes.
14. Arrange a large-sized serving platter in the middle of a wooden board. Set aside.
15. In 2 small-sized bowls, place the sour cream and fig jam respectively.
16. Arrange the bowls of sour cream and fig jam onto the platter over the board.
17. Arrange the hash browns and remaining ingredients onto the platter around the bowls and serve.

Per Serving:
Calories: 604| Fat: 44.2g| Carbs: 23.4g| Fiber: 3.5g| Protein: 27.3g

HASH BROWN & SCRAMBLED EGGS BOARD

Prep Time: 25 mins.| Cook Time: 45 mins.| Serves: 6

For Hash Brown
- Non-stick cooking spray
- 20 oz. bag hash brown potatoes, thawed
- 1 C. scallion, sliced
- ½ C. Parmesan cheese, grated
- 1 tsp. salt
- ½ tsp. ground black pepper
- 2 tbsp. olive oil

For Scrambled Eggs
- 2 tbsp. olive oil
- 1 small onion, finely chopped
- 12 large eggs, lightly beaten
- Salt and ground black pepper, as needed
- 4 oz. cheddar cheese, shredded

For Board
- ¾ C. onion jam
- ¾ C. cream cheese, softened
- 8 oz. smoked salmon
- 2 C. fresh mixed berries

1. Preheat your oven to 400 °F.
2. Grease a 12 C. muffin pan lightly with cooking spray.
3. For hash browns: with a cheesecloth, squeeze the potatoes to remove all the excess liquid.
4. With paper towels, pat dry the potatoes completely.
5. In a large-sized bowl, and add the potatoes and remaining ingredients and mix until finely blended.
6. Now, divide the muffin mixture into each prepared cup evenly and with a small-sized spoon, press each C. slightly.
7. Bake for approximately 45 minutes.
8. Meanwhile, foe scrambled eggs: heat oil in a large-sized, heavy-bottomed wok over a medium heat and cook the onion for approximately 4-5 minutes.
9. Add the eggs with salt and pepper and cook for 2-3 minutes, stirring continually.
10. Remove the wok from heat and immediately, stir in the cheese.
11. Carefully remove the muffin pan from oven and place it onto a rack for 9-10 minutes.
12. Then remove the muffins from pan and place onto the wire rack.
13. Arrange a large-sized serving platter in the middle of a wooden board. Set aside.
14. In 2 small-sized bowls, place the onion jam and cream cheese respectively.
15. Arrange the bowls of onion jam and cream cheese onto the platter over the board.
16. Arrange the hash browns, scrambled eggs and remaining ingredients onto the platter around the bowls and serve.

Per Serving:
Calories: 521| Fat: 41.2g| Carbs: 32.7g| Fiber: 6.7g| Protein: 31.4g

BISCUIT & SAUSAGE GRAVY BOARD

Prep Time: 20 mins.| Cook Time: 15 mins.| Serves: 8

For Gravy
- 1 lb. bulk pork sausage
- 4-5 tbsp. unsalted butter
- 8-10 tbsp. all-purpose flour
- Salt, as needed
- 1 tsp. ground black pepper
- 5-6 C. whole milk

For Board
- 1 C. strawberry jam
- 1 C. honey
- 8 buttermilk biscuits, warmed
- 8 cooked bacon slices
- 1 C. fresh strawberries
- 1 C. fresh blueberries
- 1 C. fresh raspberries
- 1 C. fresh blackberries

1. For gravy: heat a large-sized, heavy-bottomed wok over a medium heat and cook the sausage for approximately 3-5 minutes, breaking into crumbles.
2. Drain the grease from the wok.
3. In the wok, add the butter and cook until it melts completely.

4. Stir in the flour, salt and pepper and cook for 1½-2 minutes, stirring continually.
5. Now add the milk, stirring continually and bring it to a boil.
6. Cook for 1½-2 minutes, stirring continually.
7. Transfer the gravy into a large-sized serving bowl.
8. Arrange a large-sized serving platter in the middle of a wooden board. Set aside.
9. In 2 small-sized bowls, place the strawberry jam and honey respectively.
10. Arrange the bowls of gravy, strawberry jam and honey onto the platter over the board.
11. Arrange the biscuits and remaining ingredients onto the platter around the bowls and serve.

Per Serving:
Calories: 920| Fat: 43.2g| Carbs: 105.5g| Fiber: 3.1g| Protein: 30.1g

VEGAN BISCUIT & GRAVY BOARD

Prep Time: 25 mins.| Cook Time: 18 mins.| Serves: 6

For Biscuits
- ✓ 1 C. unsweetened almond milk
- ✓ 1 tbsp. fresh lemon juice
- ✓ 2½ C. unbleached all-purpose flour
- ✓ 1 tbsp. baking powder
- ✓ ½ tsp. baking soda
- ✓ Pinch of salt
- ✓ 4 tbsp. chilled coconut oil
- ✓ 1-2 tbsp. olive oil

For Gravy
- ✓ 5 tbsp. olive oil
- ✓ 7 tbsp. all-purpose flour
- ✓ ½ tsp. lemon-pepper seasoning
- ✓ 1/8 tsp. ground nutmeg
- ✓ Pinch of garlic powder
- ✓ 4 C. almond milk
- ✓ Salt and ground black pepper, as needed

For Board
- ✓ 1 C. hummus
- ✓ 1 C. pesto
- ✓ 1 C. marinated olives
- ✓ 1 C. roasted chickpeas
- ✓ 2 C. cherry tomatoes, halved
- ✓ 2 C. fresh baby greens

1. For biscuits: preheat your oven to 425 °F.
2. Arrange a rack in the center of oven.
3. Line a cookie sheet with baking paper.
4. In a mug, blend the cashew milk and lemon juice. Set aside for approximately 10 minutes.
5. In a medium-sized bowl, put flour, salt, baking soda and baking powder and bled well.
6. With a pastry cutter, cut in the coconut milk until a crumbly mixture forms.
7. Add in the cashew milk mixture and mix with wooden spoon until just blended.
8. Place the dough onto a floured, smooth surface and with your lightly floured hands, pat it into a (1-inch) thick circle.
9. With your floured fingers, gently flatten the dough into ¾-inch thickness.
10. With a 2½-inch floured cookie cutter, cut in the biscuits.
11. Place the biscuits onto the prepared cookie sheet.
12. Brush the top of biscuits with olive oil lightly.
13. Bake for approximately 15-18 minutes.
14. Meanwhile, for gravy: heat oil in a medium-sized saucepan over a medium-high heat and cook the flour for approximately 2-3 minutes, stirring continually.
15. Add the seasoning, nutmeg and garlic powder and stir to blend.
16. Now, add the milk, stirring continually and bring to a gentle simmer.
17. Now, set the heat to medium and cook for 9-10 minutes, stirring frequently.
18. Add in salt and black pepper and remove the pan of gravy from heat.
19. Transfer the gravy into a large-sized glass bowl.
20. Remove the biscuits from oven and set them aside for approximately 10-15 minutes before serving.
21. Arrange a large-sized serving platter in the middle of a wooden board. Set aside.
22. In 2 small-sized bowls, place the hummus and pesto respectively.
23. Arrange the bowls of gravy, hummus and pesto onto the platter over the board.
24. Arrange the biscuits and remaining ingredients onto the platter around the bowls and serve.

Per Serving:
Calories: 760| Fat: 41.9g| Carbs: 82.6g| Fiber: 12.3g| Protein: 21g

CREPES & BACON BOARD

Prep Time: 20 mins.| Cook Time: 24 mins.| Serves: 6

For Crepes
- ✓ 6 oz. cream cheese, softened
- ✓ 6 tbsp. Parmesan cheese, grated
- ✓ 6 large eggs
- ✓ 1 tsp. white sugar
- ✓ 1½ tbsp. coconut flour
- ✓ 1/8 tsp. xanthan gum
- ✓ 2 tbsp. unsalted butter

For Board
- ✓ 6 tbsp. whipped cream
- ✓ 6 tbsp. strawberry preserves
- ✓ 6 tbsp. Nutella
- ✓ 12 cooked bacon slices
- ✓ 1 C. fresh blueberries
- ✓ 1 C. fresh raspberries
- ✓ 1 C. fresh blackberries
- ✓ 1 C. seedless green grapes

1. For crepes: in a clean blender, add cream cheese, Parmesan cheese, eggs and sugar and process on low speed until finely blended.
2. While the motor is running, place the coconut flour and xanthan gum and process until a thick mixture is formed.
3. Now, pulse on medium speed for a few seconds.
4. Then place the crepe mixture into a bowl and set it aside for 3-5 minutes.
5. Divide the mixture into 12 equal-sized portions.
6. Melt the butter in a non-stick crepe pan over a medium-low heat.
7. Place 1 portion of the crepe mixture into the crepe pan and spread it in a thin layer.
8. Cook for 1½ minutes or until the edges become brown.
9. Carefully change the side of cooked crepe and cook for 20-30 seconds further.
10. Cook the remaining crepes in the same way.
11. Arrange a large-sized serving platter in the middle of a wooden board. Set aside.
12. In 3 small-sized bowls, place the whipped cream, strawberry preserves and Nutella respectively.
13. Arrange the bowls of whipped cream, strawberry preserves and Nutella onto the platter over the board.
14. Arrange the crepes, bacon, berries and grapes around the bowls and serve.

Per Serving:
Calories: 798| Fat: 54.9g| Carbs: 42.7g| Fiber: 5.4g| Protein: 33.9g

CREPES & FRUIT BOARD
Prep Time: 20 mins.| Cook Time: 48 mins.| Serves: 8

For Crepes
- ✓ 4 tbsp. unsalted butter, melted
- ✓ 8 eggs
- ✓ 4 tsp. white sugar
- ✓ ¼ tsp. sea salt
- ✓ 8 tbsp. coconut flour
- ✓ 1½ C. heavy cream
- ✓ Non-stick cooking spray

For Board
- ✓ ½ C. fig jam
- ✓ ½ C. chocolate sauce
- ✓ 8 hard-boiled eggs, peeled and halved
- ✓ 2 large bananas, peeled and sliced
- ✓ 2 apples, cored and sliced
- ✓ 2 C. fresh mixed berries

1. For crepes: in a mixing bowl, add butter, eggs, sugar, and salt, and whisk until finely blended.
2. Slowly, add the flour, beating continually until finely blended.
3. Now, place the heavy cream and whisk until blended completely.
4. Grease a heavy-bottomed wok with cooking spray lightly and then heat over a medium heat.
5. Add the desired amount of crepe mixture and spread it in a thin layer.
6. Cook for 3 minutes, flipping once after 2 minutes.
7. Cook the remaining crepes in the same way.
8. Arrange a large-sized serving platter in the middle of a wooden board. Set aside.
9. In 2 small-sized bowls, place the jam and chocolate sauce respectively.
10. Arrange the bowls of whipped jam and chocolate sauce onto the platter over the board.
11. Arrange the crepes and remaining ingredients onto the platter around the bowls and serve.

Per Serving:
Calories: 611| Fat: 26.7g| Carbs: 81g| Fiber: 8.5g| Protein: 14.9g

CREPES & TOFU SCRAMBLE BOARD
Prep Time: 25 mins.| Cook Time: 64 mins.| Serves: 8

For Crepes
- ✓ 2 C. white whole-wheat flour
- ✓ ½ tsp. salt
- ✓ 4 eggs
- ✓ 1 C. whole milk
- ✓ 1 C. water
- ✓ 2 tbsp. olive oil

For Tofu Scramble
- ✓ 2 tbsp. olive oil
- ✓ 2 large onions, finely chopped
- ✓ 2 large bell peppers, seeded and finely chopped
- ✓ 4 C. cherry tomatoes, finely chopped
- ✓ 6 C. firm tofu, crumbled and chopped
- ✓ ½ tsp. cayenne powder
- ✓ ¼ tsp. ground turmeric
- ✓ Sea salt, as needed

For Board

- 2 tbsp. olive oil
- 8 C. fresh spinach
- Salt and ground black pepper, as needed
- 1 C. cream cheese, softened
- 8 thin ham slices
- 1 C. cheddar cheese, shredded

1. For crepes: in a bowl, blend together flour and salt.
2. In the bowl of flour mixture, place the eggs and mix until finely blended.
3. Now, add milk and water and whisk until finely blended.
4. Heat olive oil in a heavy-bottomed wok over a medium-high heat.
5. Add the desired amount of crepe mixture and spread it in a thin layer.
6. Cook for 1½-2 minutes.
7. Carefully flip the side and cook for 1-2 minutes.
8. Cook the remaining crepes in the same way.
9. Meanwhile, for tofu scramble: heat oil in a large-sized wok, over a medium heat and cook the onion and bell pepper for approximately 4-5 minutes.
10. Stir in the chopped tomatoes and cook for 1-2 minutes.
11. Add in the tofu, turmeric, cayenne powder and salt and cook for 7-8 minutes.
12. For spinach: heat oil in a large-sized, heavy-bottomed wok over a medium heat and cook spinach for approximately 3-4 minutes or until wilted.
13. Stir in salt and black pepper and immediately remove the wok from heat.
14. Arrange a large-sized serving platter in the middle of a wooden board. Set aside.
15. In a small-sized bowl, place the cream cheese.
16. Arrange the bowl of cream cheese onto the platter over the board.
17. Arrange the crepes and remaining ingredients onto the platter around the bowl serve.

Per Serving:
Calories: 613| Fat: 39.1g| Carbs: 38g| Fiber: 8g| Protein: 34.9g

PANCAKES, BACON & SAUSAGE BOARD
Prep Time: 20 mins.| Cook Time: 24 mins.| Serves: 6

For Pancakes
- ½ C. whole-wheat flour
- ½ C. all-purpose flour
- 2 tsp. baking powder
- ¼ tsp. sea salt
- 1 small egg
- ½ C. plus 1 tbsp. whole milk
- 2 tbsp. olive oil
- 2 tbsp. brown sugar
- ½ tsp. ground cinnamon
- ½ tsp. vanilla extract
- ½ C. apple, cored and grated

For Board
- 1/3 C. maple syrup
- 1/3 C. unsalted butter, softened
- 6 cooked breakfast sausage links
- 12 cooked bacon slices
- 6 hard-boiled eggs, peeled and halved
- 2 oranges, peeled and sectioned
- 1 C. seedless green grapes
- 1 C. fresh strawberries, hulled and halved
- 1 C. kiwi fruit, peeled and chopped
- 1/3 C. almonds
- 1/3 C. pecans
- 1/3 C. dried apricots
- 1/3 C. dried figs

1. For pancakes: in a large-sized bowl, blend together both flours with baking powder and salt.
2. In another medium-sized bowl, add the remaining ingredients except for apples and whisk until finely blended.
3. Add the apples and stir to blend.
4. In the bowl of flour mixture, add the apple mixture and mix with wooden spoon until just blended.
5. Set the mixture aside for approximately 22-30 minutes.
6. Heat a lightly greased cast-iron wok over a medium-low heat.
7. Place about ¼ C. of the pancake mixture and cook for 1½-2 minutes per side.
8. Cook the remaining pancakes in the same way.
9. Arrange a large-sized serving platter in the middle of a wooden board. Set aside.
10. In 2 small-sized bowls, place the maple syrup and butter respectively.
11. Arrange the bowls of maple syrup and butter onto the platter over the board.
12. Arrange the pancakes and remaining ingredients onto the platter around the bowls and serve.

Per Serving:
Calories: 917| Fat: 58.1g| Carbs: 62.9g| Fiber: 5.7g| Protein: 38.7g

PANCAKES, BACON & BERRIES BOARD
Prep Time: 20 mins.| Cook Time: 40 mins.| Serves: 8

For Pancakes
- 8 eggs

- 1 C. ricotta cheese
- ½ C. vanilla whey protein powder
- 1 tsp. baking powder
- ¼ tsp. salt
- 1 tsp. liquid stevia
- 4 tbsp. unsalted butter

For Board
- ½ C. strawberry yogurt
- ½ C. maple syrup
- 16 cooked bacon slices
- 8 hard-boiled eggs, peeled and halved
- 4 C. fresh mixed berries
- 1 C. mixed nuts

1. For pancakes: in a clean blender, add all the ingredients and process until finely blended.
2. Melt the butter in a heavy-bottomed wok over a medium heat.
3. Add the desired amount of pancake mixture and spread it evenly.
4. Cook for 2-3 minutes.
5. Flip the pancake and cook for 1-2 minutes.
6. Cook the remaining pancakes in the same way.
7. Arrange a large-sized serving platter in the middle of a wooden board. Set aside.
8. In 2 small-sized bowls, place the yogurt and maple syrup respectively.
9. Arrange the bowls of yogurt and maple syrup onto the platter over the board.
10. Arrange the pancakes and remaining ingredients onto the platter around the bowls and serve.

Per Serving:
Calories: 777| Fat: 52g| Carbs: 32.9g| Fiber: 3.5g| Protein: 45.2g

PANCAKES, SAUSAGE & VEGGIE BOARD
Prep Time: 20 mins.| **Cook Time:** 64 mins.| **Serves:** 8

For Pancakes
- 8 C. zucchinis, shredded
- Salt, as needed
- ½ C. cooked chicken, shredded
- ½ C. scallion, finely chopped
- 2 eggs, beaten
- ½ C. coconut flour
- Ground black pepper, as needed
- 2 tbsp. olive oil

For Board
- ½ C. sour cream
- ½ C. unsalted butter, softened
- 16 cooked breakfast sausage links
- 8 soft-boiled eggs, peeled
- 2 C. cherry tomatoes, halved
- 2 C. sautéed mushrooms

1. For pancakes: in a colander, add zucchini and sprinkle with salt.
2. Set aside for approximately 8-10 minutes.
3. Squeeze the zucchinis well and transfer into a bowl.
4. In a bowl, add squeezed zucchini and remaining ingredients and mix until finely blended.
5. Heat oil in a large-sized heavy-bottomed wok over a medium heat.
6. In the heated wok, add ¼ C. of zucchini mixture and then shape it into an even circle.
7. Cook for 3-4 minutes per side.
8. Cook the remaining pancakes in the same way.
9. Arrange a large-sized serving platter in the middle of a wooden board. Set aside.
10. In 2 small-sized bowls, place the sour cream and butter respectively.
11. Arrange the bowls of sour cream and butter onto the platter over the board.
12. Arrange the pancakes and remaining ingredients onto the platter around the bowls and serve.

Per Serving:
Calories: 402| Fat: 28.3g| Carbs: 14.8g| Fiber: 6.8g| Protein: 23.1g

WAFFLES, BACON & SALMON BOARD
Prep Time: 20 mins.| **Cook Time:** 32 mins.| **Serves:** 8

For Waffles
- ½ C. almond flour
- 2 tbsp. coconut flour
- 2 tsp. mixed dried herbs
- 1 tsp. baking powder
- ½ tsp. garlic powder
- ½ tsp. onion powder
- Salt and ground black pepper, as needed
- ½ C. cream cheese, softened
- 6 large eggs
- 1 C. cheddar cheese, grated
- ¾ C. Parmesan cheese, grated
- Non-stick cooking spray

For Board
- ½ C. sour cream
- ½ C. cream cheese, softened
- ½ C. honey mustard
- 8 fried eggs
- 8 cooked bacon slices
- 8 oz. smoked salmon
- 2 C. fresh baby arugula

1. For waffles: in a bowl, blend together the flours, dried herbs, baking powder and seasoning and mix until finely blended.
2. In a separate bowl, put cream cheese and eggs and whisk until finely blended.
3. Add the flour mixture, cheddar cheese and Parmesan cheese and mix until finely blended.
4. Preheat your waffle maker and then lightly spray it with cooking spray.
5. After preheating, place the desired amount of waffle mixture into your waffle maker and cook for 3-4 minutes.
6. Cook the remaining waffles in the same way.
7. Arrange a large-sized serving platter in the middle of a wooden board. Set aside.
8. In 3 small-sized bowls, place the sour cream, honey mustard and cream cheese respectively.
9. Arrange the bowls of sour cream, honey mustard and cream cheese onto the platter over the board.
10. Arrange the waffles and remaining ingredients onto the platter around the bowls and serve.

Per Serving:
Calories: 603| Fat: 44.5g| Carbs: 12.8g| Fiber: 2.1g| Protein: 36.9g

---

WAFFLES & SCRAMBLED EGGS BOARD
Prep Time: 20 mins.| Cook Time: 40 mins.| Serves: 8

For Waffles
- Non-stick cooking spray
- 4 large egg, beaten
- 4 C. ricotta cheese, crumbled
- 4 C. mozzarella cheese, shredded
- 1 C. Parmesan cheese, grated
- 16 oz. frozen spinach, thawed and squeezed well
- 4 garlic cloves, finely minced
- Salt and ground black pepper, as needed

For Scrambled Eggs
- 8 eggs
- ½ tsp. red pepper flakes
- Salt and ground black pepper, as needed
- ½ C. fresh basil, chopped
- 1 C. tomatoes, chopped
- 2 tbsp. olive oil

For Board
- ½ C. whipped cream
- ½ C. unsalted butter, melted
- 16 cooked bacon slices
- 2 C. mozzarella cheese
- 4 C. fresh baby greens

1. For waffles: preheat your waffle maker and then lightly spray it with cooking spray.
2. In a medium-sized bowl, put all ingredients and with a fork, mix until finely blended.
3. After preheating, place the desired amount of waffle mixture into your waffle maker and cook for 4-5 minutes.
4. Cook the remaining waffles in the same way.
5. Meanwhile, for egg scramble: in a large-sized bowl, add eggs, red pepper flakes, salt and black pepper and beat well.
6. Add basil and tomatoes and stir to blend.
7. Heat oil in a large-sized heavy-bottomed wok over a medium-high heat.
8. Add in the beaten egg mixture and cook for 4-5 minutes, stirring continually.
9. Arrange a large-sized serving platter in the middle of a wooden board. Set aside.
10. In 2 small-sized bowls, place the whipped cream and butter respectively.
11. Arrange the bowls of whipped cream and butter onto the platter over the board.
12. Arrange the waffles, scrambled eggs and remaining ingredients onto the platter around the bowls and serve.

Per Serving:
Calories: 848| Fat: 64.2g| Carbs: 12.6g| Fiber: 1.8g| Protein: 56.2g

---

WAFFLES & BACON BOARD
Prep Time: 20 mins.| Cook Time: 32 mins.| Serves: 8

For Waffles
- Non-stick cooking spray
- 8 tbsp. unsalted butter, melted and cooled
- 8 large eggs
- 8 oz. cream cheese, softened
- 1 C. powdered sugar
- 4 tsp. vanilla extract
- Pinch of salt
- 1 C. almond flour
- 8 tbsp. coconut flour
- 4 tsp. baking powder

For Board
- 1 C. plain Greek yogurt
- ½ C. strawberry jam
- ½ C. maple syrup
- 8 hard-boiled eggs, peeled and halved
- 16 cooked bacon slices
- ½ C. fresh strawberries
- ½ C. fresh blueberries

1. Preheat your waffle maker and then lightly spray it with cooking spray.
2. In a bowl, add the butter and eggs and whisk until creamy.
3. Add the sugar, cream cheese, vanilla extract and salt and whisk until finely blended.
4. Add the baking powder and both flours and whisk until finely blended.
5. After preheating, place ¼ of the mixture into your waffle maker and cook for 4 minutes.
6. Cook the remaining waffles in the same way.
7. Arrange a large-sized serving platter in the middle of a wooden board. Set aside.
8. In 3 small-sized bowls, place the yogurt, jam and maple syrup respectively.
9. Arrange the bowls of yogurt, jam and maple syrup onto the platter over the board.
10. Arrange the waffles, eggs, bacon and berries around the bowls and serve.

Per Serving:
Calories: 869| Fat: 64.2g| Carbs: 56.6g| Fiber: 5g| Protein: 41.6g

WAFFLES, FRUIT & ALMONDS BOARD

Prep Time: 15 mins.| Cook Time: 30 mins.| Serves: 6

For Waffles
- 1¾ C. all-purpose flour
- 1-2 tbsp. white sugar
- 2 tsp. baking powder
- ¼ tsp. salt
- 1 large egg
- 1 C. whole milk
- ½ C. ricotta cheese
- 2 tbsp. canola oil
- 2 tbsp. unsalted butter, melted
- 1 tbsp. fresh lemon juice
- 1 tbsp. lemon rind, grated
- Non-stick cooking spray

For Board
- 1/3 C. honey
- 1/3 C. plain Greek yogurt
- 1/3 C. chocolate spread
- 2 large bananas, peeled and sliced
- 1 large orange, peeled and sectioned
- ½ C. kiwi, peeled and sliced
- ½ C. persimmon, peeled and sliced
- ½ C. fresh strawberries, hulled and sliced
- ¼ C. fresh raspberries
- ¼ C. fresh blueberries
- ¼ C. pomegranate seeds
- 1/3 C. almonds

1. For waffles: add the flour, salt, 2 tbsp. of sugar and baking powder in a bowl **and** and blend it well.
2. In another bowl, add the egg, milk, ricotta cheese, oil, butter, 1 tbsp. of lemon juice and rind and whisk until finely blended.
3. In the bowl of flour mixture, add the egg mixture and mix until finely blended.
4. Preheat your waffle maker and then lightly spray it with cooking spray.
5. After preheating, place 1/3 C. of the mixture into your waffle maker and cook for 4-5 minutes.
6. Cook the remaining waffles in the same way.
7. Arrange a large-sized serving platter in the middle of a wooden board. Set aside.
8. In 3 small-sized bowls, place the yogurt, honey and chocolate spread respectively.
9. Arrange the bowls of yogurt, honey and chocolate spread onto the platter over the board.
10. Arrange the waffles and remaining ingredients onto the platter around the bowls and serve.

Per Serving:
Calories: 490| Fat: 16.6g| Carbs: 78.5g| Fiber: 5.2g| Protein: 11.5g

WAFFLES, BACON & FRUIT BOARD

Prep Time: 20 mins.| Cook Time: 30 mins.| Serves: 6

For Waffles
- 2 C. all-purpose flour
- 1 tbsp. plus 2 tsp. baking powder
- 1 tsp. ground cinnamon
- Pinch of ground nutmeg
- Pinch of ground cloves
- ¼ tsp. salt
- 2 large eggs
- 1¼ C. whole milk
- 2/3 C. plain Greek yogurt
- 2 tsp. honey
- 1 tsp. vanilla extract
- Non-stick cooking spray

For Board
- 1/3 C. honey
- 1/3 C. plain Greek yogurt
- 1 C watermelon, peeled and cut into slices
- 1 C seedless green grapes
- 2 bananas, peeled and sliced
- 1 mango, peeled, pitted and sliced
- 2 oranges, peeled and sectioned

1. For waffles: in a medium-sized bowl, blend together the flour, spices, baking powder and salt
2. In another large-sized bowl, add the remaining ingredients and whisk until finely blended.

3. Add the flour mixture and mix until finely blended and smooth.
4. Preheat your waffle maker and then lightly spray it with cooking spray.
5. After preheating, place 1/3-½ C. of the mixture into your waffle maker and cook for 4-5 minutes.
6. Cook the remaining waffles in the same way.
7. Arrange a large-sized serving platter in the middle of a wooden board. Set aside.
8. In 2 small-sized bowls, place the honey and yogurt respectively.
9. Arrange the bowls of honey and yogurt onto the platter over the board.
10. Arrange the waffles and remaining ingredients onto the platter around the bowls and serve.

Per Serving:
Calories: 417| Fat: 4.1g| Carbs: 85.9g| Fiber: 5.1g| Protein: 11.1g

BAGELS & FRUIT BOARD
Prep Time: 15 mins.| Serves: 6

BAGELS, BACON & SALMON BOARD
Prep Time: 15 mins.| Serves: 6

For Whipped Cream Cheese
- 1 C. cream cheese, softened
- ¼ C. scallions, chopped
- 1 tsp. fresh lemon juice
- Pinch of salt

For Board
- 6 bagels, cut in half
- 6 tbsp. unsalted butter, softened
- ½ lb. cooked bacon slices
- ½ lb. smoked salmon
- 2 avocados, peeled, pitted and sliced
- 1 cucumber, sliced
- 2 radishes, sliced
- 1 large tomato, sliced
- 6 hard-boiled eggs, peeled and sliced

1. Arrange a large-sized serving platter in the middle of a wooden board. Set aside.
2. For whipped cream cheese: in a medium-sized bowl, place the cream cheese and with a hand mixer, whip until fluffy and light.
3. Add in the scallion, lemon juice and salt and stir to blend.
4. Spread the butter over each bagel half evenly.
5. Arrange the bowl of whipped cream cheese onto the platter over the board.
6. Arrange the bagel halves and remaining ingredients onto the platter around the bowl serve.

- 1 C. cream cheese, softened
- 1 C. bacon jam
- 1/3 C. maple syrup
- 6 bagels
- 1 (5-oz.) package sweetened dried orange slices
- 1 C. seedless grapes
- 1 peach, pitted and sliced
- 1 apple, cored and sliced
- 2 seedless cucumbers, sliced

1. Arrange a large-sized serving platter in the middle of a wooden board. Set aside.
2. In 3 small-sized bowls, place the cream cheese, jam and maple syrup respectively.
3. Arrange the bowls of cream cheese, jam and maple syrup onto the platter over the board.
4. Arrange the bagels and remaining ingredients onto the platter around the bowls and serve.

Per Serving:
Calories: 528| Fat: 13.7g| Carbs: 88.3g| Fiber: 4.8g| Protein: 15.5g

Per Serving:
Calories: 957| Fat: 61.6g| Carbs: 61.6g| Fiber: 7.4g| Protein: 41.5g

BAGELS & OATCAKE BISCUITS BOARD
Prep Time: 15 mins.| Serves: 8

- ½ C. strawberry jam
- ½ C. unsalted butter, softened
- 8 bagels
- 8 oz. oatcake biscuits
- 8 salami slices
- 6 oz. Gouda cheese
- 6 oz. Brie cheese
- 5 oz. Boursin cheese
- 4 oz. stilton cheese
- 1 small cantaloupe, peeled and cubed
- 1 large orange, peeled and sectioned
- 8 oz. fresh strawberries
- 6 oz. fresh raspberries
- 8 hard-boiled eggs, peeled and sliced

1. Arrange a large-sized serving platter in the middle of a wooden board. Set aside.
2. In 2 small-sized bowls, place the jam and butter respectively.
3. Arrange the bowls of jam and butter onto the platter over the board.
4. Arrange the bagels and remaining ingredients onto the platter around the bowls and serve.

Per Serving:

Calories: 977 | Fat: 51.3g | Carbs: 96g | Fiber: 7.4g | Protein: 37.2g

BAGEL & DELI MEAT BOARD
Prep Time: 15 mins. | Serves: 6

- 1/3 C. unsalted butter, softened
- 1/3 C. onion jam
- 6 bagels
- 6 salami slices
- 6 prosciutto slices
- 6 cooked pork sausage links
- 6 cooked bacon slices
- 6 hard-boiled eggs, peeled and halved

FRENCH TOAST & BACON BOARD
Prep Time: 20 mins. | Cook Time: 32 mins. | Serves: 8

For French Toast
- 2 large eggs
- 1½ C. whole milk
- 3 tbsp. white sugar
- 1 tsp. ground cinnamon
- Pinch of ground nutmeg
- 2 tsp. vanilla extract
- 1 stale white bread loaf, cut into thick slices
- 4-6 tbsp. unsalted butter

For Board
- ½ C. maple syrup
- ½ C. raspberry jelly
- 16 cooked bacon slices
- 8 hard-boiled eggs, peeled and halved
- 2 C. fresh mixed berries
- ¼ C. chocolate chips

1. In a large-sized shallow dish, whisk together the milk, eggs, sugar, spices and vanilla extract.
2. Coat both sides of 2 bread slices with egg mixture.
3. Melt a little butter in a large-sized, heavy-bottomed wok over a medium heat and cook the coated bread slices for approximately 3-4 minutes per side.
4. Cook the remaining slices with butter in same manner.
5. Arrange a large-sized serving platter in the middle of a wooden board. Set aside.
6. In 2 small-sized bowls, place the maple syrup and raspberry jelly respectively.
7. Arrange the bowls of maple syrup and raspberry jelly onto the platter over the board.
8. Arrange the French toasts and remaining ingredients onto the platter around the bowls and serve.

- 3 C. mixed fruit

1. Arrange a large-sized serving platter in the middle of a wooden board. Set aside.
2. In 2 small-sized bowls, place the jam and butter respectively.
3. Arrange the bowls of jam and butter onto the platter over the board.
4. Arrange the bagels and remaining ingredients onto the platter around the bowls and serve.

Per Serving:
Calories: 919 | Fat: 42.2g | Carbs: 96.1g | Fiber: 4.7g | Protein: 40.1g

Per Serving:
Calories: 791 | Fat: 40.1g | Carbs: 71.3g | Fiber: 3.2g | Protein: 34.4g

FRENCH TOAST & FRUIT BOARD
Prep Time: 20 mins. | Cook Time: 32 mins. | Serves: 8

For French Toast
- 1 C. whole milk
- 4 eggs
- 2/3 C. white sugar
- 1/3 C. unsweetened cocoa powder
- 1/8 tsp. baking powder
- ¼ tsp. salt
- 8 white bread slices
- 3-4 tbsp. unsalted butter
- 2 tsp. cinnamon-sugar

For Board
- ½ C. apricot jam
- ½ C. whipped cream
- ½ C. honey
- 2 apples, cored and sliced
- 2 bananas, peeled and sliced
- ½ C. fresh figs, thinly sliced
- ½ C. seedless grapes
- ½ C. fresh blueberries
- ¼ C. candied walnuts

1. Put the milk, eggs, sugar, spices and vanilla extract in a large-sized shallow dish and whisk until finely blended.
2. Coat both sides of 2 bread slices with egg mixture.
3. Melt a little butter in a large-sized, heavy-bottomed wok over a medium heat and cook 2 coated bread slices for approximately 3-4 minutes per side.
4. Cook the remaining slices with butter in same manner.
5. Sprinkle the French toasts with cinnamon sugar.

6. Arrange a large-sized serving platter in the middle of a wooden board. Set aside.
7. In 3 small-sized bowls, place the apricot jam, whipped cream and honey respectively.
8. Arrange the bowls of apricot jam, whipped cream and honey onto the platter over the board.
9. Arrange the French toasts and remaining ingredients onto the platter around the bowls and serve.

Per Serving:
Calories: 437| Fat: 13.3g| Carbs: 80.4g| Fiber: 5.4g| Protein: 7.5g

FRENCH TOAST & NUTS BOARD
Prep Time: 20 mins.| Cook Time: 30 mins.| Serves: 12

For French Toast
- 6 eggs
- ½ C. whole milk
- Pinch of salt
- ½ C. unsalted butter, melted
- ¾ C. brown sugar
- 1 tbsp. ground cinnamon
- 12 sandwich bread slices

For Board
- 1 C. peanut butter spread
- 1 C. chocolate sauce
- ¾ C. maple syrup
- 1 C. coconut flakes
- ½ C. mini chocolate chips
- 1/3 C. walnuts
- 1/3 C. almonds
- 1/3 C. pistachios
- 4 C. fresh mixed berries

1. In a large-sized shallow dish, whisk together the milk, eggs and salt.
2. Place the melted butter into a 9x13-inch baking dish.
3. With a brush, grease the sides of baking dish with some butter.
4. Sprinkle the top of butter brown sugar and cinnamon evenly.
5. Arrange the bread slices on top in two layers and top with egg mixture evenly.
6. Cover the baking dish of bread slices and place in the refrigerator overnight.
7. Preheat your oven to 350 °F.
8. Uncover the baking dish and bake for approximately 30 minutes.
9. Remove the baking dish of French toast from oven and set it aside for 8-10 minutes before serving.
10. Arrange a large-sized serving platter in the middle of a wooden board. Set aside.
11. In 3 small-sized bowls, place the peanut butter spread, chocolate sauce and maple syrup respectively.
12. Arrange the bowls of peanut butter spread, chocolate sauce and maple syrup onto the platter over the board.
13. Arrange the French toasts and remaining ingredients onto the platter around the bowls and serve.

Per Serving:
Calories: 581| Fat: 31.7g| Carbs: 62.5g| Fiber: 5.1g| Protein: 15.3g

FRENCH TOAST, BACON & SALMON BOARD
Prep Time: 20 mins.| Cook Time: 24 mins.| Serves: 8

- ½ C. chickpea flour
- 6 tbsp. onion, finely chopped
- 4 tsp. green chili, seeded and finely chopped
- 1 tsp. red chili powder
- ½ tsp. ground turmeric
- ½ tsp. ground cumin
- Salt, as needed
- Water, as needed
- 8 white bread slices
- 4-6 tbsp. unsalted butter

For Board
- 1 C. sour cream
- 1 C. warm cheese sauce
- 16 cooked bacon slices
- 8 oz. smoked salmon
- 8 fried eggs
- 2 C. microgreens

1. For French toast: add all the ingredients except for bread slices and butter in a large-sized shallow dish and mix until a thick mixture forms.
2. Coat 2 bread slices with chickpea flour mixture evenly.
3. Melt a little butter in a large-sized heavy-bottomed wok over a medium heat and cook 2 coated bread slices for approximately 2-3 minutes per side.
4. Cook the remaining slices with butter in same manner.
5. Arrange a large-sized serving platter in the middle of a wooden board. Set aside.
6. In 2 small-sized bowls, place the sour cream and cheese sauce respectively.
7. Arrange the bowls of sour cream and cheese sauce onto the platter over the board.

8. Arrange the French toasts and remaining ingredients onto the platter around the bowls and serve.

Per Serving:
Calories: 690| Fat: 50.7g| Carbs: 23.9g| Fiber: 3.7g| Protein: 37.1g

FRENCH TOAST, HAM & SAUSAGE BOARD
Prep Time: 20 mins.| Cook Time: 36 mins.| Serves: 6

For French Toast
- 1 C. whole milk
- 5 large eggs
- 1 garlic clove, minced
- 2 tsp. fresh chives, thinly sliced
- 1 tsp. fresh oregano, minced
- 1 tsp. fresh thyme, minced
- 2 tbsp. whole-grain mustard
- 1 tsp. ground coriander
- ½ tsp. ground cumin
- ½ tsp. paprika
- Salt and ground black pepper, as needed
- 6 French bread slices
- 4 tbsp. unsalted butter

For Board
- ¾ C. unsalted butter, softened
- ½ C. yogurt tzatziki
- 6 fried eggs
- 6 ham slices
- 6 cooked breakfast sausage links
- 2 C. fresh baby greens

1. For French toast: whisk together the milk, eggs, garlic, herbs, mustard, spices, salt, and pepper into a shallow dish.
2. Coat both sides of 2 bread slices with egg mixture.
3. Melt a little butter in a large-sized heavy-bottomed wok over a medium heat and cook 2 coated bread slices for approximately 2-3 minutes per side.
4. Cook the remaining slices with butter in same manner.
5. Arrange a large-sized serving platter in the middle of a wooden board. Set aside.
6. In 2 small-sized bowls, place the butter and yogurt tzatziki respectively.
7. Arrange the bowls of butter and yogurt tzatziki onto the platter over the board.
8. Arrange the French toasts and remaining ingredients onto the platter around the bowls and serve.

Per Serving:

Calories: 684| Fat: 57.5g| Carbs: 12.3g| Fiber: 1g| Protein: 29.2g

CROISSANT, HAM & SALAMI BOARD
Prep Time: 15 mins.| Serves: 6

- 1/3 C. smoked salmon dip
- 1/3 C. honey mustard
- 12 mini croissants
- 6 soft-boiled eggs, peeled
- 12 black forest ham slices, cut into smaller pieces
- 2 oz. salami slices
- 4 oz. Brie cheese
- 2 C. fresh cherries
- 2 C. fresh strawberries, hulled
- 1 orange, peeled and sectioned

1. Arrange a large-sized serving platter in the middle of a wooden board. Set aside.
2. In 2 small-sized bowls, place the salmon dip and honey mustard respectively.
3. Arrange the bowls of salmon dip and honey mustard onto the platter over the board.
4. Arrange the remaining ingredients onto the platter around the bowls and serve.

Per Serving:
Calories: 689| Fat: 35.9g| Carbs: 61.5g| Fiber: 5.6g| Protein: 29.1g

CROISSANT BOARD
Prep Time: 15 mins.| Serves: 6

- 1 C. vanilla yogurt
- ½ C. strawberry jam
- 1/3 C. maple syrup
- 12 mini croissants
- 6 hard-boiled eggs, peeled and halved
- 12 cooked bacon slices
- 6 oz. smoked salmon
- 1 C. fresh strawberries
- ½ C. fresh blueberries
- ½ C. fresh blackberries

1. Arrange a large-sized serving platter in the middle of a wooden board. Set aside.
2. In 3 small-sized bowls, place the yogurt, strawberry jam and maple syrup respectively.
3. Arrange the bowls of yogurt, strawberry jam and maple syrup onto the platter over the board.
4. Arrange the remaining ingredients onto the platter around the bowls and serve.

Per Serving:

Calories: 741| Fat: 35.6g| Carbs: 76.2g| Fiber: 3.6g| Protein: 29.2g

MUFFINS, FRUIT & ALONDS BOARD
Prep Time: 15 mins.| Cook Time: 12 mins.| Serves: 6

For Muffins
- Non-stick cooking spray
- 2 C. all-purpose flour
- 3 tsp. baking powder
- ¼ tsp. salt
- 6 tbsp. smooth peanut butter
- 4 tbsp. olive oil
- 1½ C. whole milk
- 6 tbsp. honey

For Boards
- ¾ C. cool whip
- ¾ C. strawberry jam
- 2 C. mixed fruit
- 1/3 C. chocolate chips
- 1/3 C. almonds, chopped

1. Preheat your oven to 350 °F.
2. Grease a 12 cups standard-sized muffin pan lightly with cooking spray.
3. In a large-sized bowl, add the flour, salt and baking powder and mix until finely blended.
4. Add the peanut butter and oil in the bowl with flour mixture and with a fork, mix until a crumbly mixture forms.
5. Add the honey and milk and mix with wooden spoon until just blended.
6. Now, divide the muffin mixture into each prepared cup evenly.
7. Bake for approximately 10-12 minutes.
8. Carefully remove the muffin pan from oven and place it onto a rack for 9-10 minutes.
9. After 10 minutes, remove each muffin from cups and place them onto a large-sized plate to cool before serving.
10. Arrange a large-sized serving platter in the middle of a wooden board. Set aside.
11. In 2 small-sized bowls, place the cool whip and strawberry jam respectively.
12. Arrange the bowls of cool whip and strawberry jam onto the platter over the board.
13. Arrange the muffins and remaining ingredients onto the platter around the bowls and serve.

Per Serving:
Calories: 671| Fat: 27.7g| Carbs: 99.2g| Fiber: 4.8g| Protein: 13.5g

MUFFINS & CITRUS FRUIT BOARD
Prep Time: 15 mins.| Cook Time: 30 mins.| Serves: 6

For Muffins
- Non-stick cooking spray
- 1 C. all-purpose flour
- 1 C. whole-wheat flour
- 1 tsp. baking soda
- 1 tsp. ground cinnamon
- 1/8 tsp. salt
- 4 bananas, peeled and mashed
- 1 egg
- 1 C. unsweetened almond milk
- ½ C. coconut oil, melted
- 1 tsp. vanilla extract
- ½ tsp. almond extract

For Board
- 6 oz. cream cheese, softened
- 4 oz. strawberry preserves
- 8 oz. seedless grapes
- 2 oranges, peeled and sectioned
- 2 grapefruit, peeled and sectioned
- 2 bananas, peeled and sliced

1. Preheat your oven to 325 °F.
2. Grease a 12 cups standard-sized muffin pan lightly with cooking spray.
3. In a bowl, add the flours, cinnamon, baking soda and salt and mix until finely blended.
4. In another bowl, add the bananas, egg, almond milk, coconut oil and both extracts and whisk until finely blended.
5. Add the flour mixture and mix with wooden spoon until just blended.
6. Now, divide the muffin mixture into each prepared cup evenly.
7. Bake for approximately 26-30 minutes.
8. Carefully remove the muffin pan from oven and place it onto a rack for 9-10 minutes.
9. After 10 minutes, remove each muffin from cups and place them onto a large-sized plate to cool before serving.
10. Arrange a large-sized serving platter in the middle of a wooden board. Set aside.
11. In 2 small-sized bowls, place the cream cheese and strawberry preserves respectively.
12. Arrange the bowls of cream cheese and strawberry preserves onto the platter over the board.
13. Arrange the muffins and remaining ingredients onto the platter around the bowls and serve.

Per Serving:
Calories: 664| Fat: 30.9g| Carbs: 91.9g| Fiber: 9.2g| Protein: 11.2g

MUFFINS & BERRIES BOARD

Prep Time: 20 mins.| Cook Time: 22 mins.| Serves: 6

For Muffins
- ¾ C. raisins
- Non-stick cooking spray
- 2 C. blanched almond flour
- ½ C. unsweetened shredded coconut
- 1 tsp. baking soda
- ½ tsp. ground allspice
- ½ tsp. ground ginger
- ¼ tsp. salt
- 3 eggs
- ½ C. honey
- ½ C. coconut oil, melted
- 1 C. carrot, peeled and grated
- 2 tbsp. fresh ginger, peeled and grated

For Board
- 1 C. mango jam
- 1/3 C. maple syrup
- 2 C. fresh mixed berries
- 1 banana, peeled and sliced

1. Soak the raisins in a bowl of cold water for 12-15 minutes.
2. Then drain the raisins well.
3. Preheat your oven to 350 °F.
4. Grease a 12 cups standard-sized muffin pan lightly with cooking spray.
5. In a large-sized bowl, add the flour, coconut shreds, baking soda, spices and salt and mix until finely blended.
6. In another bowl, add the coconut oil, eggs and honey and whisk until finely blended.
7. Add the flour mixture and mix with wooden spoon until just blended.
8. Gently fold in the carrot, ginger and raisins.
9. Now, divide the muffin mixture into each prepared cup evenly.
10. Bake for approximately 20-22 minutes.
11. Carefully remove the muffin pan from oven and place it onto a rack for 9-10 minutes.
12. After 10 minutes, remove each muffin from cups and place them onto a large-sized plate to cool before serving.
13. Arrange a large-sized serving platter in the middle of a wooden board. Set aside.
14. In 2 small-sized bowls, place the mango jam and maple syrup respectively.
15. Arrange the bowls of mango jam and maple syrup onto the platter over the board.
16. Arrange the muffins and remaining ingredients onto the platter around the bowls and serve.

Per Serving:
Calories: 770| Fat: 42.9g| Carbs: 88.7g| Fiber: 7.3g| Protein: 3.8g

MUFFINS, BACON & HASH BROWNS BOARD

Prep Time: 20 mins.| Cook Time: 25 mins.| Serves: 6

For Muffins
- 2 C. self-rising flour
- ½ of vegetable stock cube, crumbled
- Salt and ground black pepper, as needed
- 2 medium eggs, beaten slightly
- ½ C. unsalted butter, melted
- ½ C. whole milk
- 2 C. cheddar cheese, grated
- 2 C. fresh baby spinach, chopped
- ½ of bell pepper, seeded and chopped
- 1 scallion, chopped

For Board
- 1 C. apricot jam
- 1 C. sour cream
- 6 cooked bacon slices
- 12 oz. cooked hashbrowns
- 2 C. fresh baby greens

1. Preheat your oven to 350 °F.
2. Line a 12 cups standard-sized muffin pan with paper liners.
3. For muffins: in a bowl, add the flour, stock cube, salt and black pepper and mix until finely blended.
4. In another large-sized bowl, add the butter, eggs and milk and mix until finely blended.
5. Add the cheese, spinach, bell pepper and scallion and stir to blend.
6. Add the flour mixture and mix with wooden spoon until just blended.
7. Now, divide the muffin mixture into each prepared cup evenly.
8. Bake for approximately 20-25 minutes.
9. Carefully remove the muffin pan from oven and place it onto a rack for 9-10 minutes.
10. After 10 minutes, remove each muffin from cups. Arrange a large-sized serving platter in the middle of a wooden board. Set aside.
11. In 2 small-sized bowls, place the apricot jam and sour cream respectively.
12. Arrange the bowls of apricot jam and sour cream onto the platter over the board.
13. Arrange the muffins and remaining ingredients onto the platter around the bowls and serve.

Per Serving:
Calories: 895| Fat: 55g| Carbs: 71.5g| Fiber: 2.9g| Protein: 29.7g

MUFFINS, KIELBASA & SALMON BOARD
Prep Time: 20 mins.| Cook Time: 20 mins.| Serves: 6

For Muffins
- 1 egg
- 1 C. whole milk
- 3 tbsp. unsalted butter, melted
- 2 C. self-rising flour
- 1 carrot, peeled and grated
- 1 tbsp. fresh chives, chopped
- ½ C. cheddar cheese, grated
- ½ C. mozzarella cheese, grated

For Board
- 1 C. onion jam
- 1 C. sour cream
- 6 oz. smoked turkey kielbasa
- 6 oz. smoked salmon
- 3 oranges, peeled and sliced

1. Preheat your oven to 350 °F.
2. Line a 12 cups standard-sized muffin pan with paper liners.
3. In a large-sized bowl, add the egg, milk and butter and whisk until finely blended.
4. Add the flour and mix with wooden spoon until just blended.
5. Gently fold in the carrot, chives and cheeses.
6. Now, divide the muffin mixture into each prepared cup evenly.
7. Bake for approximately 16-20 minutes or until tops become golden brown.
8. Carefully remove the muffin pan from oven and place it onto a rack for 9-10 minutes.
9. After 10 minutes, remove each muffin from cups. Arrange a large-sized serving platter in the middle of a wooden board. Set aside.
10. In 2 small-sized bowls, place the onion jam and sour cream respectively.
11. Arrange the bowls of onion jam and sour cream onto the platter over the board.
12. Arrange the muffins and remaining ingredients onto the platter around the bowls and serve.

Per Serving:
Calories: 572| Fat: 28.3g| Carbs: 59.3g| Fiber: 6.3g| Protein: 20.7g

APPLE PORRIDGE BOARD
Prep Time: 15 mins.| Cook Time: 5 mins.| Serves: 8

For Porridge
- 4 C. unsweetened almond milk
- 6 tbsp. walnuts, chopped
- 6 tbsp. sunflower seeds
- 4 large apples, peeled, cored and grated
- 1 tsp. vanilla extract
- ½ tsp. ground cinnamon

For Board
- 1 C. strawberry preserves
- 1 C. maple syrup
- 2 bananas, peeled and sliced
- 1 C. fresh blueberries
- 1 C. fresh raspberries
- ½ C. walnuts
- ½ C. chocolate chips

1. In a large-sized saucepan, blend together the milk, walnuts, sunflower seeds, grated apple, vanilla and cinnamon over a medium-low heat and cook for 3-5 minutes.
2. Remove the pan of porridge from heat and transfer it into a large-sized serving bowl.
3. Arrange a large-sized serving platter in the middle of a wooden board. Set aside.
4. In 2 small-sized bowls, place the strawberry preserves and maple syrup respectively.
5. Arrange the bowls of apple porridge, strawberry preserves and maple syrup onto the platter over the board.
6. Arrange the remaining ingredients onto the platter around the bowls and serve.

Per Serving:
Calories: 469| Fat: 12.3g| Carbs: 89.4g| Fiber: 7.1g| Protein: 5.2g

QUINOA PORRIDGE BOARD
Prep Time: 15 mins.| Cook Time: 20 mins.| Serves: 8

For Porridge
- 2 C. uncooked red quinoa, rinsed and drained
- 4 C. water
- 1 tsp. vanilla extract
- 1 C. whole milk
- ½ tsp. fresh lemon peel, grated finely
- 12-15 drops liquid stevia
- 2 tsp. ground cinnamon
- 1 tsp. ground ginger
- 1 tsp. ground nutmeg

For Board
- 1½ C. warm whole milk
- ½ C. peanut butter

- ✓ 2 C. mixed berries
- ✓ 1 large apple, cored and sliced
- ✓ 1 C. mixed nuts

1. For quinoa porridge: in a large-sized saucepan, blend together the quinoa, water, and vanilla extract over a medium heat and bring it to a boil.
2. Now, set the heat to low and simmer, covered for approximately 15 minutes or until all the liquid is absorbed, stirring periodically.
3. In the pan with the quinoa, add the coconut milk, lemon peel, stevia, and spices and stir to blend.
4. Immediately remove the pan of quinoa from heat and set it aside, covered for 4-5 minutes.
5. Uncover the pan and with a fork, fluff the quinoa.
6. Place the quinoa porridge into a large-sized serving bowl.
7. Arrange a large-sized serving platter in the middle of a wooden board. Set aside.
8. In 2 small-sized bowls, place the milk and peanut butter respectively.
9. Arrange the bowls of quinoa porridge, milk and peanut butter onto the platter over the board.
10. Arrange the remaining ingredients onto the platter around the bowls and serve.

Per Serving:
Calories: 440| Fat: 22.7g| Carbs: 47.2g| Fiber: 7.3g| Protein: 11.3g

OATS & FRUIT BOARD

Prep Time: 15 mins.| **Cook Time:** 10 mins.| **Serves:** 8

For Oatmeal
- ✓ 4 C. water
- ✓ 2 C. old-fashioned oats
- ✓ ½ tsp. ground cinnamon

For Board
- ✓ 1 C. warm whole milk
- ✓ ½ C. plain Greek yogurt
- ✓ ½ C. peanut butter
- ✓ 4 tbsp. fruit spread
- ✓ 4 tbsp. honey
- ✓ 4 tbsp. maple syrup
- ✓ 2 bananas, sliced
- ✓ 1 large apple, cored and chopped
- ✓ 1 C. fresh blueberries
- ✓ 1 C. fresh strawberries, hulled
- ✓ ½ C. coconut chips, toasted
- ✓ ½ C. dried apricots
- ✓ ½ C. granola
- ✓ ¼ C. candied walnuts
- ✓ ¼ C. pistachios

1. For oatmeal: in a medium-sized saucepan, add the water over a medium heat and bring it to a boil.
2. Add in oats and cook for 3-5 minutes, stirring frequently.
3. Remove the pan of oats from heat and immediately stir in the cinnamon.
4. Transfer the oatmeal into a large-sized bowl and set aside.
5. Arrange a large-sized serving platter in the middle of a wooden board. Set aside.
6. In 6 small-sized bowls, place the milk, yogurt, peanut butter, fruit spread, honey and maple syrup respectively.
7. Arrange the bowls of oatmeal, milk, yogurt, peanut butter, fruit spread, honey and maple syrup onto the platter over the board.
8. Arrange the remaining ingredients onto the platter around the bowls and serve.

Per Serving:
Calories: 434| Fat: 20.1g| Carbs: 69.9g| Fiber: 7.8g| Protein: 13.4g

OATMEAL & MUFFINS BOARD

Prep Time: 20 mins.| **Cook Time:** 20 mins.| **Serves:** 6

For Oatmeal
- ✓ 3 C. unsweetened almond milk
- ✓ 3 C. rolled oats
- ✓ 3 tbsp. unsweetened cocoa powder
- ✓ 10-15 drops liquid stevia

For Muffins
- ✓ Non-stick cooking spray
- ✓ 1/3 C. whole-wheat flour
- ✓ ½ tsp. baking powder
- ✓ ½ tsp. ground cinnamon
- ✓ ¼ tsp. baking soda
- ✓ 1/8 tsp. salt
- ✓ ½ C. old-fashioned oats
- ✓ 3 tsp. white sugar
- ✓ 1 small egg
- ✓ ½ C. unsweetened applesauce
- ✓ ¼ C. whole milk
- ✓ 2 tbsp. coconut oil, melted

For Board
- ✓ ½ C. cranberry sauce
- ✓ ½ C. maple syrup
- ✓ 1 C. fresh mixed berries
- ✓ 1 apple, cored and sliced
- ✓ 1 banana, peeled and sliced
- ✓ ½ C. dried apricots
- ✓ ½ C. chocolate chips

- ✓ 1/3 C. almonds

1. For oatmeal: put all ingredients in a large-sized container and mix until finely blended.
2. Cover the container and place in the refrigerator overnight.
3. Preheat your oven to 375 °F.
4. Grease 6 cups of a muffin pan lightly with cooking spray.
5. For muffins: place the flour, cinnamon, baking powder, baking soda, and salt in a large-sized bowl and mix until finely blended.
6. In another bowl, add the oats, sugar, egg, applesauce, milk, coconut oil and vanilla extract and whisk until finely blended.
7. Add the oat mixture in the bowl with flour mixture and with a wooden spoon, mix until just blended.
8. Now, divide the muffin mixture into each prepared cup evenly.
9. Bake for approximately 16-20 minutes.
10. Carefully remove the muffin pan from oven and place it onto a rack for 9-10 minutes.
11. After 10 minutes, remove each muffin from cups and place them onto a large-sized plate to cool before serving.
12. Arrange a large-sized serving platter in the middle of a wooden board. Set aside.
13. In 2 small-sized bowls, place the cranberry sauce and maple syrup respectively.
14. Arrange the bowls of oatmeal, cranberry sauce and maple syrup onto the platter over the board.
15. Arrange the muffins and remaining ingredients onto the platter around the bowls and serve.

Per Serving:
Calories: 533| Fat: 18.2g| Carbs: 86.7g| Fiber: 10.6g| Protein: 11.5g

LUNCH, DINNER & SNACKS BOARDS

ORANGE & OLIVES BOARD
Prep Time: 15 mins. | Serves: 8

- 1 C. corn salsa
- 1 C. guacamole
- 12 oz. Queso fresco, sliced
- 8 oz. Manchego cheese, sliced
- 6 oz. Queso Chihuahua, sliced
- 1 C. pimento-stuffed green olives
- 4 mandarin oranges, peeled and sliced
- ½ C. pecans, halved
- 8 ham slices
- 4 oz. fish crackers

1. Arrange a large-sized serving platter in the middle of a wooden board. Set aside.
2. In 2 small-sized bowls, place the guacamole and salsa respectively.
3. Arrange the bowls of guacamole and salsa onto the platter over the board.
4. Arrange remaining ingredients onto the platter around the bowl serve.

Per Serving:
Calories: 392| Fat: 24g| Carbs: 27.1g| Fiber: 4.3g| Protein: 17.8g

VEGGIES BOARD
Prep Time: 15 mins. | Serves: 8

- 1 C. hummus
- 1 C. plain Greek yogurt
- 12 oz. macadamia nut cheese, sliced
- 2 carrots, peeled and cut into sticks
- 1 cucumber, sliced
- 2 C. cherry tomatoes, halved
- 1 C. black olives, pitted
- 1 C. seedless black grapes
- ½ C. walnuts
- 8 whole-wheat pita breads, cut into triangles

1. Arrange a large-sized serving platter in the middle of a wooden board. Set aside.
2. In 2 small-sized bowls, place the hummus and plain Greek yogurt respectively.
3. Arrange the bowls of hummus and plain Greek yogurt onto the platter over the board.
4. Arrange the remaining ingredients onto the platter around the bowl serve.

Per Serving:
Calories: 439| Fat: 16g| Carbs: 61.4g| Fiber: 8.9g| Protein: 18.4g

DELI MEAT, FRUIT & CHEESE BOARD
Prep Time: 15 mins. | Serves: 8

- ½ C. fig jam
- 1 C. pimento-stuffed olives
- 4 oz. Brie cheese, sliced
- 4 oz. blue cheese, cubed
- 2 C. mature cheddar cheese, cubed
- 16 black forest ham slices
- 16 salami slices
- 3 C. seedless green grapes
- 16 baby figs, halved
- ½ C. salted walnuts
- 32 salty crackers

1. Arrange a large-sized serving platter in the middle of a wooden board. Set aside.
2. In a small-sized bowl, place the fig jam.
3. Arrange the bowls of fig jam onto the platter over the board.
4. Arrange remaining ingredients onto the platter around the bowl serve.

Per Serving:
Calories: 759| Fat: 44.9g| Carbs: 60.7g| Fiber: 6.7g| Protein: 31.1g

SALMON & VEGGIES BOARD
Prep Time: 15 mins.| Serves: 6

- 4 oz. cream cheese, softened
- ¼ tsp. red pepper flakes
- Salt, as needed
- 12 oz. smoked salmon
- 3 oz. feta cheese, cubed
- 1 cucumber, thinly sliced
- 1 bell pepper, seeded and thinly sliced
- 1 tomato, thinly sliced
- 5 radishes, thinly sliced
- 1/3 C. marinated artichoke hearts
- 1/3 C. assorted olives
- 1 small red onion, thinly sliced
- 1 lemon, cut into wedges

1. Arrange a large-sized serving platter in the middle of a wooden board. Set aside.
2. In a small-sized bowl, place the cream cheese, red pepper flakes and salt and whisk until smooth.
3. Arrange the bowl of cream cheese mixture onto the platter over the board.
4. Arrange remaining ingredients onto the platter around the bowl serve.

Per Serving:
Calories: 204| Fat: 13g| Carbs: 7.5g| Fiber: 1.7g| Protein: 14.9g

SALMON & FRUIT BOARD
Prep Time: 15 mins.| Serves: 6

- 14 oz. smoked salmon
- 4 oz. mozzarella cheese balls
- 2 C. cheddar crackers
- 1 watermelon, peeled and sliced s
- 1 cantaloupe, seeded and thinly sliced
- 1 large mango, peeled, pitted and sliced
- 2 C. seedless grapes
- 4 kiwi, peeled and sliced
- 2 apples, cored and sliced

1. Arrange a large-sized serving platter in the middle of a wooden board. Set aside.
2. In a small-sized bowl, place the cream cheese, red pepper flakes and salt and whisk until smooth.
3. Arrange the bowl of cream cheese mixture onto the platter over the board.
4. Arrange remaining ingredients onto the platter around the bowl serve.

Per Serving:
Calories: 322| Fat: 9.1g| Carbs: 45.2g| Fiber: 5.6g| Protein: 21.3g

TABBOULEH & AVOCADO BOARD
Prep Time: 15 mins.| Serves: 6

For Tabbouleh
- 1 C. uncooked bulgur
- 4 C. hot vegetable broth
- 4-6 Roma tomatoes, cored and chopped
- 4-6 C. fresh parsley leaves, chopped
- 1 C. fresh mint leaves, chopped
- ½ C. scallions, chopped
- 4 tbsp. olive oil
- 4 tbsp. fresh lemon juice
- 1 tsp. salt

For Board
- ¾ C. hummus
- 2 large avocados, peeled, pitted and sliced
- 1 C. Kalamata olives, pitted
- 6 pita breads, cut into triangles

- ✓ 1½ C. feta cheese, cubed

1. For tabbouleh: in a large-sized bowl, add the bulgur and broth and set aside, covered for approximately 30-60 minutes or until softened.
2. Through a fine-mesh strainer, strain the bulgur and transfer into a large-sized serving bowl.
3. In the bowl of bulgur, add the tomatoes and remaining ingredients and mix until finely blended.
4. Arrange a large-sized serving platter in the middle of a wooden board. Set aside.
5. In a small-sized bowl, place the hummus.
6. Arrange the bowls of tabbouleh and hummus onto the platter over the board.
7. Arrange the remaining ingredients onto the platter around the bowls and serve.

Per Serving:
Calories: 699| Fat: 38.1g| Carbs: 72.2g| Fiber: 16.1g| Protein: 23.2g

VEGGIES & YOGURT BOARD

Prep Time: 20 mins.| Cook Time: 4 mins.| Serves: 10

- ✓ 1 C. walnuts
- ✓ 1 lb. Persian cucumbers, sliced
- ✓ ¾ tsp. salt, divided
- ✓ 1 tbsp. fresh basil, shredded
- ✓ 1 garlic clove, crushed
- ✓ ½ tsp. lemon zest, grated
- ✓ 1 tbsp. olive oil
- ✓ ½ tsp. ground pepper
- ✓ 3 C. plain Greek yogurt, whipped
- ✓ 2 tbsp. unsalted butter
- ✓ 1 bunch baby carrots, halved lengthwise
- ✓ 8 oz. green beans
- ✓ 8 oz. multi-coloured bell peppers, seeded and sliced
- ✓ 2 C. cherry tomatoes
- ✓ 4 radishes, thinly sliced
- ✓ 8 oz. Gouda cheese, thinly sliced
- ✓ 8 oz. aged sharp cheddar cheese, cut into ½-inch cubes

1. In a large-sized bowl of water, soak the walnuts for approximately 5 hours.
2. Drain the walnuts and rinse them under cold running water.
3. Again, place the walnuts in the bowl of fresh water and place in the refrigerator overnight.
4. Again, drain the walnuts and pat them dry with paper towels.
5. Then chop the walnuts roughly. Set aside.
6. In a large-sized bowl, place the cucumber slices and sprinkle with ¼ tsp. of salt.
7. With a potato masher, mash the cucumbers until juicy.
8. Place the mashed cucumber into a colander and set aside to drain for approximately 5 minutes.
9. Transfer the drained cucumber into a large-sized bowl and stir in basil, garlic, lemon zest, oil, black pepper and remaining salt.
10. In a medium-sized bowl, place the yogurt and top with cucumber mixture and walnuts.
11. Arrange a large-sized serving platter in the middle of a wooden board. Set aside.
12. Place the bowl of yogurt onto the platter over the board.
13. Melt the butter in a small-sized wok over a medium heat for approximately 2-4 minutes, stirring continually.
14. Immediately remove the wok from heat and drizzle over the cucumbers.
15. Arrange the veggies and cheeses around the bowl of yogurt.
16. Serve with the garnishing of remaining basil.

Per Serving:
Calories: 379| Fat: 26g| Carbs: 17.4g| Fiber: 4.3g| Protein: 20.5g

BEANS & POTATO BOARD

Prep Time: 20 mins.| Cook Time: 30 mins.| Serves: 6

For Baked Potatoes
- ✓ 2 lb. red potatoes, cut into ½-inch cubes
- ✓ ¼ C. olive oil
- ✓ ½ tsp. paprika
- ✓ ½ tsp. garlic powder
- ✓ ½ tsp. onion powder
- ✓ Salt and ground black pepper, as needed

For Board
- ✓ 1 tbsp. olive oil
- ✓ 6 cooked breakfast sausage links
- ✓ 1 C. salsa

- ✓ 1 C. guacamole
- ✓ 1 C. Pico de Gallo
- ✓ 6 soft-boiled eggs, peeled and halved
- ✓ 12 cooked bacon slices
- ✓ 1½ C. baked beans
- ✓ 6 corn tortillas, warmed
- ✓ 2 large avocados, peeled, pitted and sliced
- ✓ ¾ C. Cotija cheese
- ✓ ¾ C. cheddar cheese, shredded
- ✓ 1½ C. mango, peeled, pitted and cubed
- ✓ 3-4 tbsp. fresh cilantro, chopped
- ✓ 2 jalapeño peppers, sliced

1. Preheat your oven to 450 °F.
2. Grease a large-sized rimmed cookie sheet.
3. For potatoes: in a large-sized bowl, put all ingredients and toss to blend.
4. Place the potato cubes onto the prepared cookie sheet and then arrange them in an even layer.
5. Bake for approximately 30 minutes, flipping the potatoes once halfway through.
6. Now set the oven to broiler and arrange the oven rack about 5-inch from heating element.
7. Broil the potatoes for approximately 2-3 minutes.
8. Meanwhile, heat oil in a large-sized heavy-bottomed wok over a medium-low heat and cook the sausage links for approximately 15-16 minutes, stirring frequently.
9. Remove the sausage links from wok and place onto a paper towel-lined dish.
10. Remove the potatoes from oven and set them aside for approximately 4-5 minutes.
11. Arrange a large-sized serving platter in the middle of a wooden board. Set aside.
12. In 3 small-sized bowls, place the salsa, guacamole and Pico de Gallo respectively.
13. Arrange the bowls of salsa, guacamole and Pico de Gallo onto the platter over the board.
14. Arrange the potatoes, sausage links and remaining ingredients onto the platter around the bowls and serve.

Per Serving:
Calories: 927| Fat: 63.3g| Carbs: 58.5g| Fiber: 12.6g| Protein: 36g

TUNA & VEGGIES BOARD
Prep Time: 15 mins.| Cook Time: 19 mins.| Serves: 6

- ✓ 12 oz. small red potatoes
- ✓ 10 oz. fresh green beans, trimmed
- ✓ 1 (15-oz.) can water-packed tuna, drained and flaked
- ✓ 6 oz. small tomatoes, cut into wedges
- ✓ 1/3 C. pearl onions, quartered
- ✓ 3 garlic cloves, minced
- ✓ 1 tsp. paprika
- ✓ ¾ tsp. ground cumin
- ✓ ½ tsp. red pepper flakes, crushed
- ✓ Salt and ground black pepper, as needed
- ✓ 1/3 C. olive oil
- ✓ 3 tbsp. white wine vinegar
- ✓ 6 oz. unsalted butter lettuce

1. In a large-sized pan of water, cook the potatoes over a medium-high heat and bring it to a boil.
2. Cook for 10 minutes.
3. With a spoon, transfer the potatoes onto a plate.
4. Place the green beans in the same pan of water and cook for 4 minutes.
5. Remove the pan of green beans from heat and drain them.
6. Immediately place the drained green beans into the bowl of iced water for approximately 5 minutes.
7. Again, drain the green beans and with paper towels, pat dry them.
8. Cut each potato in half lengthwise.
9. Arrange a large-sized serving platter in the middle of a wooden board. Set aside.
10. In a large-sized bowl, add the potatoes, green beans and remaining ingredients except for lettuce and toss to blend.
11. Arrange the lettuce onto the platter over the board and top with the tuna mixture.
12. Serve immediately.

Per Serving:
Calories: 250| Fat: 12.2g| Carbs: 15.8g| Fiber: 3.9g| Protein: 20.6g

PEPPERONI & CHICKPEAS BOARD
Prep Time: 15 mins.| Serves: 12

- ✓ 2 (15-oz.) cans chickpeas, drained
- ✓ 1 (3½-oz.) package sliced pepperoni
- ✓ 1 (24-oz.) jar pepperoncini peppers, drained
- ✓ 2 C. fresh mushrooms, halved
- ✓ 2 C. cherry tomatoes, halved
- ✓ 1 (6-oz.) can pitted ripe olives, drained
- ✓ ½ lb. provolone cheese, cubed
- ✓ 6 C. lettuce, torn
- ✓ 6 C. fresh baby spinach
- ✓ 1 (8-oz.) bottle Italian vinaigrette dressing

1. Arrange a large-sized serving platter in the middle of a wooden board. Set aside.
2. In a large-sized bowl, place the chickpeas.
3. Arrange the bowl of chickpeas onto the platter over the board.
4. Arrange the remaining ingredients except for dressing around the bowl.

5. Drizzle with dressing and serve immediately.

Per Serving:
Calories: 430| Fat: 17g| Carbs: 51.61g| Fiber: 13.8g| Protein: 21.7g

DELI MEAT & OLIVES BOARD
Prep Time: 15 mins.| Serves: 8

- 1 C. sour cream
- 8 salami slices
- 8 Ham slices
- 8 mortadella slices
- ½ lb. mozzarella cheese, cubed
- 16 olives
- 16 cornichons
- 16 radishes
- 4 tbsp. olive oil
- Ground black pepper, as needed

1. Arrange a large-sized serving platter in the middle of a wooden board. Set aside.
2. In a small-sized bowl, place the sour cream.
3. Arrange the bowl of sour cream onto the platter over the board.
4. Arrange the remaining ingredients onto the platter around the bowl drizzle with oil.
5. Sprinkle with black pepper and serve.

Per Serving:
Calories: 345| Fat: 28.9g| Carbs: 7.9g| Fiber: 2.2g| Protein: 14.5g

DELI MEAT & BOCCONCINI BOARD
Prep Time: 20 mins.| Serves: 20

- 1 lb. bocconcini
- 1½ tbsp. olive oil
- 1 tbsp. fresh parsley, chopped
- ½ tsp. red pepper flakes, crushed
- Salt and ground black pepper, as needed
- 2 large radicchio heads, separated into leaves
- 1 lb. provolone cheese, cubed
- 1 lb. Pecorino cheese, cubed
- ¾ lb. salami, thinly sliced
- ¾ lb. prosciutto, very thinly sliced
- ¾ lb. refrigerator-dried soppressata, thinly sliced
- ¾ lb. air-dried soppressata, thinly sliced
- 2 C. roasted red peppers, drained and sliced
- 2 C. artichoke hearts, drained and quartered
- 2 C. pepperoncini peppers, drained
- 2 C. mixed olives, drained
- 10 fresh figs, halved lengthwise

1. Arrange a large-sized serving platter in the middle of a wooden board. Set aside.
2. In a large-sized bowl, blend together the bocconcini, olive oil, parsley, red pepper flakes, salt and pepper. Set aside.
3. Arrange the radicchio leaves onto the platter over the board.
4. Arrange the remaining ingredients over radicchio leaves.
5. Top with bocconcini mixture and serve.

Per Serving:
Calories: 533| Fat: 36.8g| Carbs: 13.8g| Fiber: 2.6g| Protein: 37.5g

DELI MEAT & FRUIT BOARD
Prep Time: 15 mins.| Serves: 8

- ✓ 1 C. romesco sauce
- ✓ ½ C. quince jam
- ✓ 8 Serrano ham slices
- ✓ 4 cured chorizo sausage links, sliced
- ✓ 5 oz. goat cheese, cubed
- ✓ 6 oz. Manchego cheese, cubed
- ✓ 5 oz. Iberico cheese, cubed
- ✓ 3 oz. Cabrales cheese, cubed
- ✓ 4 C. seedless grapes
- ✓ 8 dates, pitted
- ✓ 8 fresh figs, halved
- ✓ 1 C. mixed olives
- ✓ ¼ C. pickled jalapeño peppers
- ✓ ½ C. almonds
- ✓ 1 large baguette bread loaf, cut into slices
- ✓ 1 tbsp. paprika

1. Arrange a large-sized serving platter in the middle of a wooden board. Set aside.
2. In 2 small-sized bowls, place the romesco sauce and quince jam respectively.
3. Arrange the bowls of romesco sauce and quince jam onto the platter over the board.
4. Arrange the remaining ingredients onto the platter around the bowls.
5. Sprinkle with paprika and serve.

Per Serving:
Calories: 753| Fat: 43.8g| Carbs: 67g| Fiber: 7.9g| Protein: 27.9g

PICKLES & FRUIT BOARD
Prep Time: 15 mins.| Serves: 10

- ✓ ½ C. olive oil
- ✓ ½ C. Dijon mustard
- ✓ 2-3 tbsp. fresh rosemary, minced
- ✓ Salt and ground black pepper, as needed
- ✓ 1 (10-oz.) box breadsticks
- ✓ 1 C. Kalamata olives
- ✓ ½ C. dill pickles
- ✓ 1 (6-oz.) jar marinated artichoke hearts, drained
- ✓ 1 (12-oz.) jar pickled vegetables
- ✓ ½ C. olive oil-packed sun-dried tomatoes, drained
- ✓ 1 pear, cored and sliced
- ✓ 1 apple, cored and sliced
- ✓ ½ C. dates, pitted
- ✓ ¼ C. almonds
- ✓ ¼ C. cashews
- ✓ ¼ C. hazelnuts
- ✓ ¼ C. pine nuts
- ✓ 2 C. feta cheese, crumbled

1. Arrange a large-sized serving platter in the middle of a wooden board. Set aside.
2. In a bowl, add oil, mustard, rosemary, salt and pepper and whisk until finely blended.
3. Arrange the bowl of mustard sauce onto the platter over the board.
4. Arrange the remaining ingredients around he bowl and serve.

Per Serving:
Calories: 432| Fat: 27.6g| Carbs: 39.1g| Fiber: 5.5g| Protein: 11.1g

DELI MEAT & ARTICHOKE BOARD
Prep Time: 15 mins.| Serves: 12

- ✓ 3-4 tbsp. olive oil
- ✓ 2 tbsp. fresh parsley leaves, chopped
- ✓ Pinch of red pepper flakes, crushed
- ✓ 6 oz. prosciutto, sliced
- ✓ 6 oz. salami, thinly sliced
- ✓ 3 oz. pepperoni, thinly sliced
- ✓ 8 oz. bocconcini
- ✓ 8 oz. Parmesan cheese, cubed
- ✓ 8 oz. provolone cheese, thinly sliced
- ✓ 8 oz. Asiago cheese, thinly sliced
- ✓ 1 C. marinated artichoke hearts, drained
- ✓ 1 C. mixed olives, pitted and sliced
- ✓ ½ C. peppadew peppers
- ✓ ½ C. almonds
- ✓ 1 focaccia bread loaf, toasted and sliced

1. Arrange a large-sized serving platter in the middle of a wooden board. Set aside.
2. In a small-sized bowl, blend together the oil, parsley and red pepper flakes.
3. Arrange the bowl of oil mixture onto the platter over the board.
4. Arrange the remaining ingredients around he bowl and serve.

Per Serving:
Calories: 507| Fat: 32.8g| Carbs: 23g| Fiber: 1.6g| Protein: 30.7g

SALAMI & PEPPERONI BOARD
Prep Time: 15 mins.| Serves: 8

- ✓ 1 C. fig jam
- ✓ 8 oz. salami
- ✓ 4 oz. pepperoni
- ✓ 4 oz. Brie cheese
- ✓ 4 oz. cheddar cheese, cubed
- ✓ 2 granny Smith apples, cored and sliced
- ✓ 3 oz. thin crisp crackers
- ✓ 1½ C. C. seedless red grapes
- ✓ 1½ C. seedless green grapes
- ✓ 1 C. pomegranate arils
- ✓ 1 C. dragon fruit, peeled and sliced
- ✓ ½ C. pistachios
- ✓ ½ C. pecans
- ✓ ¼ C. dried figs
- ✓ ¼ C. dried cranberries
- ✓ ¼ C. dried apricots
- ✓ ¼ C. dried dates

1. Arrange a large-sized serving platter in the middle of a wooden board. Set aside.
2. In a small-sized bowl, place the fig jam.
3. Arrange the bowl of fig jam onto the platter over the board.
4. Arrange the remaining ingredients onto the platter around the bowl serve.

Per Serving:
Calories: 635| Fat: 32.1g| Carbs: 73.7g| Fiber: 6.9g| Protein: 17.8g

DELI PORK MEAT BOARD
Prep Time: 15 mins.| Serves: 8

- ✓ 3 tbsp. olive oil
- ✓ 2 tbsp. balsamic vinegar
- ✓ 2 tsp. fresh basil leaves, minced
- ✓ 2 tsp. fresh parsley leaves, minced
- ✓ ¼ tsp. ground black pepper
- ✓ 8 Salami slices
- ✓ 8 cured pork shoulder slices
- ✓ 8 Ham slices
- ✓ 8 mortadella slices
- ✓ 9 oz. mozzarella cheese, sliced
- ✓ 1 C. black olives, pitted and sliced
- ✓ 1 C. bell pepper, seeded and sliced
- ✓ 1 C. cherry tomatoes, quartered

1. Arrange a large-sized serving platter in the middle of a wooden board. Set aside.
2. In a small-sized bowl, add oil, vinegar, fresh herbs and black pepper and mix until finely blended.
3. Arrange the remaining ingredients onto the platter over the board.
4. Drizzle with oil mixture and serve.

Per Serving:
Calories: 420| Fat: 32.3g| Carbs: 6.3g| Fiber: 1.4g| Protein: 27.4g

DELI MEAT & SALMON BOARD
Prep Time: 15 mins.| Serves: 8

For Whipped Ricotta
- ✓ 1 C. ricotta cheese
- ✓ 1-2 tbsp. olive oil
- ✓ 2 tsp. lemon zest, grated
- ✓ Pinch of salt

For Board
- ✓ 8 oz. Italian assorted meats (prosciutto, calabrese salami, capocollo, bresaola)
- ✓ 6 oz. smoked salmon
- ✓ 8 oz. mozzarella cheese, cubed
- ✓ 16 breadsticks
- ✓ 6 oz. marinated artichoke hearts, drained
- ✓ 5 oz. mixed olives, pitted and sliced
- ✓ 5 oz. pepperoncini peppers, drained
- ✓ 5 oz. roasted red peppers, drained
- ✓ 6 oz. cherry peppers, drained
- ✓ 1 large heirloom tomato, chopped

1. For whipped ricotta: in a small-sized bowl, put all ingredients and with a wire whisk, beat until smooth.
2. Arrange a large-sized serving platter in the middle of a wooden board. Set aside.
3. Arrange the bowl of whipped ricotta onto the platter over the board.
4. Arrange the remaining ingredients onto the platter around the bowl of whipped ricotta and serve.

Per Serving:
Calories: 316| Fat: 17.2g| Carbs: 18.5g| Fiber: 3.1g| Protein: 22g

CALAMARI BOARD
Prep Time: 20 mins.| Cook Time: 30 mins.| Serves: 6

For Calamari
- ✓ 1½ lb. frozen calamari tubes, thawed
- ✓ 3 large eggs
- ✓ ½ C. all-purpose flour
- ✓ Pinch of salt and ground black pepper
- ✓ 2 C. Italian seasoned panko breadcrumbs

For Board
- ✓ 1 C. marinara sauce
- ✓ 1 C. sweet orange sauce
- ✓ 6 C. lettuce, torn
- ✓ 3 C. cherry tomatoes
- ✓ 2 lemons, cut into wedges

1. Preheat your oven to 400 °F.
2. Line 2 rimmed cookie sheets with baking paper.
3. For calamari: in a shallow dish, add the flour, salt and pepper and blend thoroughly.
4. In a second shallow dish, put the eggs and with a wire whisk, beat well.
5. Place the breadcrumbs.in a third shallow dish.
6. Coat the squid rings with flour lightly, then dip into eggs and finally coat with breadcrumbs.
7. Divide the squid rings onto both prepared cookie sheets evenly.
8. Bake for approximately 16-20 minutes.
9. Flip the rings and bake for approximately 10 minutes.

10. Remove both cookie sheets of calamari from oven and set aside to cool slightly.
11. Arrange a large-sized serving platter in the middle of a wooden board. Set aside.
12. In 2 small-sized bowls, place the marinara sauce and orange sauce respectively.
13. Arrange the bowls of sauces onto the platter over the board.
14. Arrange the calamari and remaining ingredients onto the platter around the bowls and serve.

Per Serving:
Calories: 439| Fat: 10.5g| Carbs: 50.8g| Fiber: 4.2g| Protein: 15.2g

POTATO & OLIVES BOARD
Prep Time: 20 mins.| Cook Time: 20 mins.| Serves: 6

- 2 lb. small new potatoes, scrubbed
- Salt, as needed
- 1 bunch fresh cilantro, roughly chopped
- ½ C. tahini
- ¼ C. fresh lemon juice
- 2 tbsp. water
- 2 tbsp. fresh parsley, chopped
- 2 tsp. olive oil
- 1 C. ketchup
- 1 C. sour cream
- 2 large cucumbers, cut into sticks
- 1 C. cherry tomatoes
- 1 C. bell peppers, seeded and cut into sticks
- 1 C. mixed olives

1. Arrange a large-sized serving platter in the middle of a wooden board. Set aside.
2. In a large-sized saucepan of salted water, add the potatoes over high heat and bring it to a boil.
3. Now, set the heat to low and simmer for approximately 13-15 minutes.
4. Remove the saucepan of potatoes from heat and set aside to cool in the water for approximately 1½-2 hours.
5. Drain the potatoes and cut each in half.
6. Transfer the potatoes into a large-sized bowl.
7. In a clean blender, add the cilantro, tahini, lemon juice and water and process until finely blended and smooth.
8. In the bowl of potatoes, add the parsley, salt and tahini mixture and toss to blend.
9. In 2 small-sized bowls, place the ketchup and sour cream respectively.
10. Arrange the bowls of ketchup and sour cream onto the platter over the board
11. Arrange the potatoes and remaining ingredients onto the platter around the bowls and serve.

Per Serving:
Calories: 413| Fat: 23.3g| Carbs: 47.7g| Fiber: 7.6g| Protein: 9.3g

DELI MEAT & FOUR CHEESES BOARD
Prep Time: 20 mins.| Serves: 12

- 1 C. sour cream
- ½ C. honey
- ½ C. fig jam
- 12 oz. fresh mozzarella cheese balls
- 8 oz. Brie cheese
- 6 oz. manchego cheese, cut into thin slices
- 8 oz. cheddar cheese, cubed
- 8 oz. triple cream cheese
- 8 oz. salami
- 2 oz. dried coppa
- 2 oz. prosciutto
- 1/3 C. kalamata olives, pitted
- 1/3 C. green olives, pitted
- 1 C. baby dill pickles
- 2 C. seedless grapes
- 1 apple, cored and sliced
- 1 pear, cored and sliced
- 2 C. fresh strawberries, hulled
- 1 C. fresh blueberries
- 1 C. walnuts
- 3 oz. dark chocolate bar, broken into bite-sized pieces
- 1 baguette bread, cut into slices and toasted
- 4 oz. artisan crackers
- 4 oz. artisan crackers

1. Arrange a large-sized serving platter in the middle of a wooden board. Set aside.
2. In 2 small-sized bowls, place the sour cream, honey and fig jam respectively.
3. Arrange the bowls of sour cream, honey and fig jam onto the platter over the board.
4. Arrange the remaining ingredients onto the platter around the bowl serve.

Per Serving:
Calories: 736| Fat: 41.1g| Carbs: 61.7g| Fiber: 6.4g| Protein: 33.2g

VEGGIES & HUMMUS BOARD
Prep Time: 15 mins.| Serves: 8

- 1 (17-oz.) container hummus
- 2 C. cherry tomatoes, halved
- 2 C. cucumbers, chopped
- 1 C. Kalamata olives, pitted
- 1 C. feta cheese, crumbled
- 1 large red onion, sliced
- 2 tbsp. fresh dill, chopped
- 8 pita breads, cut into triangles

1. Arrange a large-sized serving platter in the middle of a wooden board. Set aside.
2. In a small-sized bowl, place the hummus.
3. Arrange the bowl of hummus onto the platter over the board.
4. Arrange the remaining ingredients onto the platter around the bowl serve.

Per Serving:
Calories: 351| Fat: 12.4g| Carbs: 47.7g| Fiber: 6.4g| Protein: 1.3.8g

DELI MEAT & TROUT BOARD
Prep Time: 15 mins.| Serves: 8

For Whipped Ricotta
- 1½ C. ricotta cheese, drained
- ¾ tsp. kosher salt
- 1-2 tbsp. olive oil

For Board
- 8 oz. spreadable chicken liver pâté
- 1½ lb. assorted cured meats (prosciutto, salami, bresaola, mortadella, ham and soppressata)
- 4 oz. Brie cheese
- 4 oz. Manchego cheese
- 8 oz. smoked trout, skin and bones removed
- 2 bunches radishes, trimmed and halved
- 8 oz. salted almonds, roasted
- 8 oz. dried dates
- 10 oz. fig jam
- 8 oz. mixed olives
- 16 baguette bread slices, toasted

5. For whipped ricotta: in a small-sized bowl, put all ingredients and with a wire whisk, beat until smooth.
6. Arrange a large-sized serving platter in the middle of a wooden board. Set aside.
7. In 2another small-sized bowl, place the chicken liver pâté.
8. Arrange the bowls of whipped ricotta and liver pâté onto the platter over the board.
9. Arrange the remaining ingredients onto the platter around the bowls of whipped ricotta and liver pâté and serve.

Per Serving:
Calories: 725| Fat: 22g| Carbs: 84.2g| Fiber: 8.7g| Protein: 48.7g

DELI MEAT & BERRIES BOARD
Prep Time: 15 mins.| Serves: 12

- 1½ C. sour cream
- 1 C. honey
- 8 oz. Brie cheese wheel
- 4 oz. Gouda cheese, wax removed and thinly sliced
- 8 oz. cheddar cheese block, cubed
- 6 oz. pork sausage, sliced
- 6 oz. salami, thinly sliced
- 6 oz. Prosciutto, thinly sliced
- ½ C. green olives, pitted
- ½ C. Kalamata olives, pitted
- ½ C. almonds
- ¼ C. dried apricots
- 6 C. fresh mixed berries
- 8 oz. fish crackers

1. Arrange a large-sized serving platter in the middle of a wooden board. Set aside.
2. In 2 small-sized bowls, place the sour cream and honey respectively.
3. Arrange the bowls of sour cream and honey onto the platter over the board.
4. Arrange the remaining ingredients onto the platter around the bowls and serve.

Per Serving:
Calories: 598| Fat: 36.3g| Carbs: 47.5g| Fiber: 3.8g| Protein: 22.4g

CHICKEN SALAD BOARD
Prep Time: 15 mins. | Serves: 8

For Salad
- 1¾ lb. cooked chicken, chopped
- 2 C. mayonnaise
- ½ C. celery, chopped
- ½ C. dill pickles, chopped
- 2 tbsp. fresh lemon juice
- Salt and ground black pepper, as needed

For Board
- 12 C. lettuce leaves, torn
- 2 C. feta cheese, cubed
- 2 C. seedless grapes
- 2 C. artichoke hearts, drained and quartered
- 2 C. olives
- ½ C. pickled jalapeño peppers
- 1 C. oyster crackers
- 8 Hawaiian rolls

1. Arrange a large-sized serving platter in the middle of a wooden board. Set aside.
2. For salad: in a medium-sized serving bowl, put all ingredients and mix until finely blended.
3. Arrange the bowl of salad onto the platter over the board.
4. Arrange the remaining ingredients onto the platter around the bowl serve.

Per Serving:
Calories: 676 | Fat: 37.9g | Carbs: 47.2g | Fiber: 6.2g | Protein: 39.6g

SHRIMP SALAD BOARD
Prep Time: 20 mins. | Serves: 8

For Salad
- ½ C. sour cream
- 4 tbsp. mayonnaise
- 2-3 tbsp. fresh lemon juice
- 2 tsp. Old Bay seasoning
- Salt, as needed
- 2 lb. cooked shrimp
- 4 tbsp. fresh parsley, chopped

For Board
- 2 C. mozzarella cheese, cubed
- 12 C. lettuce, torn
- 2 large cucumbers, peeled and chopped
- 2 C. celery, chopped
- 2 C. tomatoes, sliced
- 2 C. pita chips
- 8 crusty bread slices, toasted

1. For salad: add sour cream, mayonnaise, lime juice, Old Bay, and salt in a large-sized salad bowl and mix until finely blended.
2. Add remaining ingredients and gently, stir to combine.
3. Refrigerate to chill before serving.
4. Arrange a large-sized serving platter in the middle of a wooden board. Set aside.
5. Arrange the bowl of salad onto the platter over the board.
6. Arrange the remaining ingredients onto the platter around the bowl serve.

Per Serving:
Calories: 319 | Fat: 9.9g | Carbs: 25g | Fiber: 2.4g | Protein: 31.9g

POTATO SALAD BOARD
Prep Time: 20 mins. | Cook Time: 25 mins. | Serves: 6

For Salad
- 4 Russet potatoes
- 6 hard-boiled eggs, peeled and chopped
- 1 C. celery, chopped
- 1 C. red onion, chopped
- 1 tbsp. Dijon mustard
- ¼ tsp. celery salt
- ¼ tsp. garlic salt
- 1 C. mayonnaise

For Board
- 4 C. fresh baby spinach
- 4 C. fresh baby arugula
- 2 C. mozzarella cheese balls
- 1 C. cucumber, sliced
- 1 C. black olives, pitted
- 1 C. oyster crackers
- 6 ciabatta bread slices, toasted

1. For salad: in a large-sized pan of water, add potatoes over high heat and bring it to a boil.
2. Now, set the heat to medium and cook for 16-20 minutes.
3. Drain the potatoes completely and transfer into a bowl.
4. Set aside to cool.
5. After cooling, chop the potatoes.
6. In a serving salad bowl, add the potatoes and remaining ingredients and gently, mix them well.
7. Refrigerate to chill before serving.
8. Arrange a large-sized serving platter in the middle of a wooden board. Set aside.
9. Arrange the bowl of salad onto the platter over the board.

10. Arrange the remaining ingredients onto the platter around the bowl serve.

Per Serving:
Calories: 478| Fat: 25g| Carbs: 51.9g| Fiber: 6.1g| Protein: 14.4g

CHICKEN SAUSAGE MEATBALLS BOARD
Prep Time: 20 mins.| Cook Time: 25 mins.| Serves: 8

For Meatloaf
- 24 oz. chicken sausage links, casings removed
- 1 C. cheddar cheese, shredded
- ½ C. buffalo sauce
- 1 C. almond flour
- 3 tbsp. coconut flour
- ½ tsp. cayenne powder
- Salt and ground black pepper, as needed

For Board
- 1 C. yogurt sauce
- 1 C. pesto
- 8 C. fresh baby spinach
- 2 cucumbers, sliced
- 2 carrots, peeled and sliced
- 2 bell peppers, seeded and sliced
- 1 C. fresh figs, sliced
- 1 C. seedless grapes
- ½ C. walnuts
- 4 oz. Havarti cheese, cubed
- 4 oz. mozzarella cheese, sliced

1. Preheat your oven to 350 °F.
2. Line 2 large cookie sheets with baking paper.
3. In a large-sized bowl, put all ingredients and mix until finely blended.
4. Make 1-inch balls from the chicken sausage mixture.
5. Arrange the balls onto both prepared cookie sheets.
6. Bake for approximately 25 minutes.
7. Remove from oven and set aside for approximately 10 minutes before serving.
8. Arrange a large-sized serving platter in the middle of a wooden board. Set aside.
9. In 2 small-sized bowls, place the yogurt sauce and pesto respectively.
10. Arrange the bowls of yogurt sauce and pesto onto the platter over the board.
11. Arrange the meatballs and remaining ingredients onto the platter around the bowls and serve.

Per Serving:
Calories: 737| Fat: 48g| Carbs: 42.9g| Fiber: 9.4g| Protein: 32.4g

PORK MEATBALLS BOARD
Prep Time: 20 mins.| Cook Time: 35 mins.| Serves: 6

For Meatballs:
- Non-stick cooking spray
- 1 lemongrass stalk, outer skin peeled and chopped
- 1 (1½-inch) piece fresh ginger, sliced
- 3 garlic cloves, chopped
- 1 C. fresh cilantro leaves, chopped roughly
- ½ C. fresh basil leaves, chopped roughly
- 2 tbsp. plus 1 tsp. fish sauce
- 2 tbsp. water
- 2 tbsp. fresh lime juice
- 1½ lb. lean ground pork
- 1 carrot, peeled and grated
- 1 egg, beaten

For Board
- ½ C. ranch dressing
- ½ C. BBQ sauce
- 2 cucumbers, sliced
- 2 carrots, peeled and sliced
- 2 bell peppers, seeded and sliced
- ½ C. radishes, sliced
- 4 oz. Havarti cheese, cubed
- 4 oz. cheddar cheese, sliced

1. Preheat your oven to 375 °F.
2. Grease a baking dish with cooking spray.
3. For meatballs: in a clean food processor, add fresh herbs, lemongrass, garlic, ginger, fish sauce, lime juice and water and process until finely chopped.
4. Transfer the blended mixture into a bowl with remaining ingredients and mix until finely blended.
5. Make about 1-inch balls from mixture.
6. Arrange the balls into the prepared baking dish in a single layer.
7. Bake for approximately 30-35 minutes.
8. Remove the baking dish of meatballs from oven and set aside for approximately 4-5 minutes.
9. Arrange a large-sized serving platter in the middle of a wooden board. Set aside.
10. In 2 small-sized bowls, place the ranch dressing and BBQ sauce respectively.
11. Arrange the bowls of ranch dressing and BBQ sauce onto the platter over the board.
12. Arrange the meatballs and remaining ingredients onto the platter around the bowls and serve.

Per Serving:
Calories: 501| Fat: 33.4g| Carbs: 19.4g| Fiber: 1.7g| Protein: 32g

LAMB MEATBALLS BOARD

Prep Time: 25 mins.| Cook Time: 15 mins.| Serves: 6

- 1 lb. lean ground lamb
- 1 egg white, beaten
- 4 fresh shiitake mushrooms, stemmed and minced
- 1 tbsp. fresh parsley, minced
- 1 tbsp. fresh basil leaves, minced
- 1 tbsp. fresh mint leaves, minced
- 2 tsp. fresh lemon zest, grated finely
- 1½ tsp. fresh ginger, grated finely
- Salt and ground black pepper, as needed

For Board
- 1 C. sour cream
- 1 C. BBQ sauce
- 6 oz. string cheese
- 8 oz. mozzarella cheese, sliced thinly
- 1 lb. baby carrots, peeled
- 2 C. grape tomatoes
- 12 breadsticks

1. Preheat your oven to 425 °F.
2. Arrange the rack in the center of oven.
3. Line a cookie sheet with baking paper.
4. In a large-sized bowl, put all ingredients and mix until finely blended.
5. Make small equal-sized balls from mixture.
6. Arrange the balls onto the prepared cookie sheet.
7. Bake for approximately 12-15 minutes.
8. Remove the baking dish of meatballs from oven and set aside for approximately 5 minutes.
9. Arrange a large-sized serving platter in the middle of a wooden board. Set aside.
10. In 2 small-sized bowls, place the sour cream and BBQ sauce respectively.
11. Arrange the bowls of sour cream and BBQ sauce onto the platter over the board.
12. Arrange the meatballs and remaining ingredients onto the platter around the bowls and serve.

Per Serving:
Calories: 797| Fat: 31.7g| Carbs: 78.1g| Fiber: 5.5g| Protein: 51.2g

BEEF MEATBALLS BOARD

Prep Time: 20 mins.| Cook Time: 30 mins.| Serves: 6

For Meatballs
- ½ C. carrot, peeled and grated
- ½ C. zucchini, grated
- ½ C. yellow squash, grated
- Salt, as needed
- 1 lb. ground beef
- 1 egg, beaten
- ¼ of a small-sized onion, finely chopped
- 1 garlic clove, minced
- 2 tbsp. fresh mixed herbs, finely chopped

For Board
- 1 C. yogurt tzatziki
- 1 C. buffalo sauce
- 6 prosciutto rolls
- 8 oz. mozzarella cheese, cubed
- 6 oz. cheddar cheese slices
- 10 C. fresh baby greens
- 2 C. olives, pitted
- 2 C. carrots, peeled and sliced
- 6 oz. pita crackers
- 4 oz. mixed nuts

1. Preheat your oven to 400 °F.
2. Line a large-sized cookie sheet with baking paper.
3. Set a large-sized colander in the sink.
4. Add carrot, zucchini and yellow squash and sprinkle with 2 pinches of salt.
5. Set aside for at least 10 minutes.
6. Transfer the veggies over a paper towel and squeeze out all the moisture of veggies.
7. In a large-sized mixing bowl, add squeezed vegetables, beef, egg, onion, garlic, herbs and desired amount of salt and mix until finely blended.
8. Make small, equal-sized balls from the beef mixture.
9. Arrange the meatballs onto the prepared cookie sheet.
10. Bake for approximately 26-30 minutes.
11. Remove the cookie sheet of meatballs from oven and set aside for approximately 5 minutes.
12. Arrange a large-sized serving platter in the middle of a wooden board. Set aside.
13. In 2 small-sized bowls, place the yogurt tzatziki and buffalo sauce respectively.
14. Arrange the bowls of yogurt tzatziki and buffalo sauce onto the platter over the board.
15. Arrange the meatballs and remaining ingredients onto the platter around the bowls and serve.

Per Serving:
Calories: 559| Fat: 26.6g| Carbs: 35.5g| Fiber: 3.8g| Protein: 44.4g

TURKEY MEATBALLS BOARD

Prep Time: 20 mins.| Cook Time: 20 mins.| Serves: 6

For Meatballs
- 1 lb. ground turkey
- 1 tbsp. olive oil

- ✓ 1 tsp. dehydrated onion flakes, crushed
- ✓ ½ tsp. granulated garlic
- ✓ ½ tsp. ground cumin
- ✓ ½ tsp. red pepper flakes, crushed
- ✓ Salt, as needed

For Board
- ✓ 1 C. marinara sauce
- ✓ 1 C. BBQ sauce
- ✓ 8 C. microgreens
- ✓ 2 C. cucumbers, sliced
- ✓ 1 C. olives, pitted
- ✓ 2 C. cherry tomatoes, halved
- ✓ 4 oz. cheddar cheese crisps
- ✓ 5 oz. fish crackers

1. Preheat your oven to 400 °F.
2. Line a large-sized cookie sheet with baking paper.
3. For meatballs: in a large-sized mixing bowl, put all ingredients and mix until finely blended.
4. Make equal-sized balls from turkey mixture.
5. Arrange the meatballs onto the prepared cookie sheet.
6. Bake for approximately 16-20 minutes.
7. Remove the cookie sheet of meatballs from oven and set aside for approximately 5 minutes.
8. Arrange a large-sized serving platter in the middle of a wooden board. Set aside.
9. In 2 small-sized bowls, place the marinara sauce and BBQ sauce respectively.
10. Arrange the bowls of marinara sauce and BBQ sauce onto the platter over the board.
11. Arrange the meatballs and remaining ingredients onto the platter around the bowls and serve.

Per Serving:
Calories: 5541| Fat: 23.5g| Carbs: 58.7g| Fiber: 6.1g| Protein: 31.6g

VEGGIE LOAF BOARD

Prep Time: 20 mins.| Cook Time: 1½ hrs.| Serves: 8

For Meatloaf
- ✓ Non-stick cooking spray
- ✓ ½ tbsp. olive oil
- ✓ 2 onions, chopped
- ✓ ½ C. celery stalk, chopped
- ✓ 1 tsp. dried rosemary, crushed
- ✓ 1 tsp. dried basil, crushed
- ✓ ¾ C. pecans, chopped
- ✓ ¾ C. walnuts, chopped
- ✓ 3 C. whole-wheat breadcrumbs
- ✓ 2½ C. unsweetened almond milk
- ✓ Salt and ground black pepper, as needed

For Board
- ✓ 1 C. yogurt sauce
- ✓ 1 C. ketchup
- ✓ 12 C. lettuce, torn
- ✓ 2 C. carrots, peeled and sliced
- ✓ 2 C. cucumbers, sliced
- ✓ 2 C. mixed nuts
- ✓ 4 C. fresh mixed berries

1. Preheat your oven to 350 °F.
2. Grease a loaf pan lightly with cooking spray.
3. In a large-sized bowl, put all ingredients and mix until finely blended.
4. Transfer the mixture into the prepared loaf pan.
5. Bake for approximately 1-1½ hours or until top become golden brown.
6. Remove the pan of meatloaf from oven and place onto a rack for approximately 9-10 minutes.
7. Then invert nut loaf onto a platter for approximately 5 minutes.
8. Cut the loaf into desired-sized slices.
9. Arrange a large-sized serving platter in the middle of a wooden board. Set aside.
10. In 2 small-sized bowls, place the yogurt sauce and ketchup respectively.
11. Arrange the bowls of yogurt sauce and ketchup onto the platter over the board.
12. Arrange the meatloaf slices and remaining ingredients onto the platter around the bowls and serve.

Per Serving:
Calories: 673| Fat: 39.3g| Carbs: 67.6g| Fiber: 10.7g| Protein: 19.1g

BEEF MEATLOAF BOARD

Prep Time: 20 mins.| Cook Time: 1¼ hrs.| Serves: 10

For Meatloaf
- ✓ Non-stick cooking spray
- ✓ 2 lb. lean ground beef
- ✓ ½ C. onion, chopped
- ✓ ½ C. bell pepper, seeded and chopped
- ✓ 2 garlic cloves, minced
- ✓ 1 C. cheddar cheese, grated
- ✓ ½ C. ketchup
- ✓ 2 eggs, beaten
- ✓ 1 tsp. dried thyme, crushed
- ✓ Salt and ground black pepper, as needed
- ✓ 3 C. fresh spinach, chopped
- ✓ 1½ C. mozzarella cheese, grated freshly

For Board
- ✓ 1 C. feta sauce
- ✓ 1 C. honey mustard

- 4 oz. mozzarella cheese
- 4 oz. Brie cheese
- 8 oz. cooked bacon, chopped
- 12 C. fresh baby greens
- 2 C. olives, pitted
- 1 C. mixed nuts
- 4 oranges, peeled and sectioned
- 2 C. figs, sliced

1. Preheat your oven to 350 °F.
2. Grease a baking dish lightly with cooking spray.
3. In a large-sized bowl, put all ingredients except spinach and mozzarella cheese and mix until finely blended.
4. Place a large-sized wax paper onto a smooth surface.
5. Place meat mixture over wax paper.
6. Place spinach over meat mixture, pressing slightly.
7. Then top the meatloaf with mozzarella cheese evenly.
8. Gently roll the wax paper around meat mixture to shape it into a meatloaf.
9. Carefully, peel the wax paper from meatloaf.
10. Place the meatloaf into the prepared baking dish.
11. Bake for approximately 1-1¼ hours.
12. Remove the baking dish of meatloaf from oven and set aside for approximately 9-10 minutes before serving.
13. Then invert nut loaf onto a platter for approximately 5 minutes.
14. Cut the loaf into desired-sized slices.
15. Arrange a large-sized serving platter in the middle of a wooden board. Set aside.
16. In 2 small-sized bowls, place the feta sauce and honey mustard respectively.
17. Arrange the bowls of feta sauce and honey mustard onto the platter over the board.
18. Arrange the meatloaf slices and remaining ingredients onto the platter around the bowls and serve.

Per Serving:
Calories: 809| Fat: 40.4g| Carbs: 59.5g| Fiber: 9.8g| Protein: 53.5g

LEMONY CHICKEN WINGS BOARD
Prep Time: 20 mins.| Cook Time: 50 mins.| Serves: 8

For Chicken Wings
- ½ C. olive oil
- ½ C. fresh lemon juice
- 6 garlic cloves, peeled and crushed
- 3-4 tsp. lemon zest, grated
- 1½ tbsp. dried oregano
- 1 tsp. paprika
- Salt and ground black pepper, as needed
- 3 lb. chicken wings

For Board
- 1 C. BBQ sauce
- 1 C. honey mustard
- 1 C. feta cheese, cubed
- 1 C. carrot, peeled and cut into sticks
- 1 C. cucumber, cut into sticks
- 1 C. celery, sliced
- 1 C. radishes, sliced
- 1 C. cherry tomatoes
- 1 C. bell peppers, seeded and cut into sticks

1. For wings: in a large-sized bowl, put all ingredients except for wings and mix until finely blended.
2. Add the wings and coat with marinade generously.
3. Refrigerate to marinate overnight.
4. Preheat your oven to 400 °F.
5. Place the chicken wings onto a large-sized cookie sheet.
6. Bake for approximately 45-50 minutes.
7. Remove the cookie sheet from oven and set aside for approximately 4-5 minutes.
8. Arrange a large-sized serving platter in the middle of a wooden board. Set aside.
9. In 2 small-sized bowls, place the BBQ sauce and honey mustard respectively.
10. Arrange the bowls of BBQ sauce and honey mustard onto the platter over the board.
11. Arrange the chicken wings and remaining ingredients onto the platter around the bowls and serve.

Per Serving:
Calories: 566| Fat: 29.6g| Carbs: 19g| Fiber: 2g| Protein: 53g

BUFFALO CHICKEN WINGS BOARD
Prep Time: 20 mins.| Cook Time: 10 mins.| Serves: 6

- 2 lb. chicken wings
- ¼ C. buffalo sauce
- 3 tbsp. unsalted butter, melted
- 1 tsp. paprika
- ½ tsp. cayenne powder
- 1/8 tsp. garlic powder
- Salt and ground black pepper, as needed

For Board
- 1 C. warm cheese sauce
- 1 C. mango chutney
- 8 C. fresh microgreens
- 2 C. mozzarella cheese balls
- 2 C. Brie cheese

- ✓ 2 C. olives, pitted
- ✓ 2 C. cherry tomatoes, halved
- ✓ ½ C. pickled jalapeño peppers

1. In a large-sized bowl, add the buffalo sauce, butter, spices, salt and pepper and mix until finely blended.
2. Reserve 2 tbsp. of marinade in a small-sized bowl.
3. In the bowl of remaining marinade, add chicken wings and toss to blend.
4. Place the bowl of wings in room temperature for approximately 28-30 minutes.
5. Preheat your oven to broiler.
6. Arrange a rack about 5-inch from heating element.
7. Remove the wings from bowl and discard the marinade.
8. Place the wings onto a broiler pan and broil for approximately 9-10 minutes per side.
9. Remove chicken wings from oven and coat with reserved marinade evenly.
10. Arrange a large-sized serving platter in the middle of a wooden board. Set aside.
11. In 2 small-sized bowls, place the cheese sauce and mango chutney respectively.
12. Arrange the bowls of cheese sauce and mango chutney onto the platter over the board.
13. Arrange the chicken wings and remaining ingredients onto the platter around the bowls and serve.

Per Serving:
Calories: 735| Fat: 40.1g| Carbs: 35.9g| Fiber: 3.1g| Protein: 59.2g

LAMB CHOPS BOARD

Prep Time: 20 mins.| Cook Time: 25 mins.| Serves: 8

For Chops
- ✓ 1 head garlic, cloves peeled
- ✓ ¼ C. fresh rosemary leaves
- ✓ ¼ C. unsalted butter, melted
- ✓ 2 (2-lb.) racks of lamb, frenched
- ✓ Salt and ground black pepper, as needed

For Board
- ✓ 1 C. yogurt sauce
- ✓ 1 C. ketchup
- ✓ ½ C. honey mustard
- ✓ 4 oz. Parmesan cheese, cubed
- ✓ 4 oz. provolone cheese, thinly sliced
- ✓ 4 oz. Asiago cheese, thinly sliced
- ✓ 2 C. bell peppers, seeded and sliced
- ✓ 2 C. marinated artichoke hearts, drained
- ✓ 1 C. olives, pitted and sliced
- ✓ ½ C. almonds
- ✓ 1 focaccia bread loaf, toasted and sliced

1. For chops: in a mini food processor, add the garlic, rosemary and butter and process until the garlic is finely chopped.
2. Rub each lamb rack with salt and pepper evenly.
3. Then rub each rack of lamb with the garlic mixture.
4. Arrange the racks of lamb onto a large-sized, rimmed cookie sheet, fat-side up.
5. Set aside for approximately 1 hour.
6. Preheat your oven to 450 °F.
7. Arrange the rack in the upper third portion of oven.
8. Bake for approximately 24-25 minutes, flipping the racks once after 16 minutes.
9. Remove from oven and place the racks onto a cutting board, stand them upright, and let rest for 10 minutes.
10. Cut each rack into individual chops.
11. Arrange a large-sized serving platter in the middle of a wooden board. Set aside.
12. In 2 small-sized bowls, place the yogurt sauce and ketchup respectively.
13. Arrange the bowls of yogurt sauce and ketchup onto the platter over the board.
14. Arrange the chops and remaining ingredients onto the platter around the bowls and serve.

Per Serving:
Calories: 850| Fat: 39.6g| Carbs: 38g| Fiber: 3.8g| Protein: 82.5g

LAMB CHOPS BOARD

Prep Time: 20 mins.| Cook Time: 8 mins.| Serves: 6

- ✓ 1 tbsp. fresh mint leaves, chopped
- ✓ 1 tsp. garlic paste
- ✓ 1 tsp. ground allspice
- ✓ ½ tsp. ground nutmeg
- ✓ ½ tsp. ground green cardamom
- ✓ ¼ tsp. hot paprika
- ✓ Salt and ground black pepper, as needed
- ✓ 4 tbsp. olive oil
- ✓ 2 tbsp. fresh lemon juice
- ✓ 2 racks of lamb, trimmed and separated into 16 chops
- ✓ Non-stick cooking spray

For Board
- ✓ 1 C. BBQ sauce
- ✓ 1 C. honey mustard
- ✓ 2 C. feta cheese, cubed
- ✓ 8 C. fresh baby greens

- ✓ 2 C. cherry tomatoes
- ✓ 1 C. carrot, peeled and cut into sticks
- ✓ 1 C. cucumber, cut into sticks
- ✓ 1 C. celery, sliced
- ✓ 1 C. olives, pitted
- ✓ 1 C. bell peppers, seeded and cut into sticks

1. For chops: in a large-sized bowl, put all of the ingredients except for chops and mix until finely blended.
2. Add the chops and mix with marinade generously.
3. Refrigerate to marinate for approximately 5-6 hours.
4. Preheat the gas grill to high heat.
5. Grease the grill grate with cooking spray.
6. Place the lamb chops onto the grill and cook for 6-8 minutes, flipping once halfway through.
7. Arrange a large-sized serving platter in the middle of a wooden board. Set aside.
8. In 2 small-sized bowls, place the yogurt sauce and honey mustard respectively.
9. Arrange the bowls of yogurt sauce and honey mustard onto the platter over the board.
10. Arrange the chops and remaining ingredients onto the platter around the bowls and serve.

Per Serving:
Calories: 800| Fat: 42.9g| Carbs: 42.9g| Fiber: 3.4g| Protein: 55.2g

SHRIMP BOARD

Prep Time: 20 mins.| Cook Time: 4 mins.| Serves: 8

- ✓ 2 lb. shrimp, peeled and deveined
- ✓ ½ of lemon
- ✓ 4 tbsp. olive oil
- ✓ 4 tbsp. red wine vinegar
- ✓ 2 tbsp. fresh parsley, chopped
- ✓ 2 tbsp. fresh basil leaves, chopped
- ✓ 2 garlic cloves, minced
- ✓ 2 tsp. lemon peel, grated
- ✓ 4 C. fresh cauliflower florets
- ✓ 2 bell peppers, seeded and cut into 1-inch pieces
- ✓ 32 Kalamata olives, pitted and halved
- ✓ 16 oz. feta cheese, cubed

1. For shrimp: in a saucepan of lightly salted boiling water, place the lemon half.
2. Then, add the shrimp and cook for 2-3 minutes, stirring frequently.
3. Remove the shrimp from pan and place into a bowl of ice water.
4. Drain the shrimp completely and then pat dry with paper towels.
5. In a large-sized bowl, add cooked shrimp, oil, vinegar, parsley, basil leaves, garlic and lemon peel and toss to blend.
6. Arrange a large-sized serving platter in the middle of a wooden board. Set aside.
7. Arrange the shrimp mixture and remaining ingredients onto the platter over the board and serve.

Per Serving:
Calories: 391| Fat: 23g| Carbs: 10.7g| Fiber: 2.3g| Protein: 35.5g

CRISPY SHRIMP BOARD

Prep Time: 25 mins.| Cook Time: 20 mins.| Serves: 6

- ✓ 3 eggs
- ✓ ½ C. panko breadcrumbs
- ✓ 1 tsp. sugar
- ✓ 1 tsp. garlic powder
- ✓ 1 tsp. onion powder
- ✓ 1/8 tsp. cayenne powder
- ✓ Salt and freshly ground white pepper, as needed
- ✓ ½ C. unsweetened coconut flakes
- ✓ 24 medium raw shrimp, peeled and deveined

For Board
- ✓ 1 C. ranch dressing
- ✓ 1 C. ketchup
- ✓ 1 C. blue cheese crumbles
- ✓ 1 C. mozzarella cheese balls
- ✓ 1 C. marinated olives
- ✓ 1 C. cherry tomatoes
- ✓ 2 oranges, peeled and sectioned
- ✓ 2 C. seedless grapes
- ✓ 1 C. figs, sliced
- ✓ 1 C. mixed nuts

1. Preheat your oven to 425 °F.
2. Line a large-sized cookie sheet with baking paper.
3. In a shallow dish, whisk the cracked eggs lightly.
4. In the second shallow dish, blend together remaining ingredients except for coconut and shrimp.
5. In a third shallow dish, put the coconut flakes.
6. First, dip the shrimp in eggs and then roll into pork rinds mixture.
7. Again dip in eggs and then roll into coconut flakes.
8. Place the shrimp onto the prepared cookie sheet.
9. Bake for approximately 16-20 minutes.
10. Arrange a large-sized serving platter in the middle of a wooden board. Set aside.
11. In 2 small-sized bowls, place the ranch dressing and ketchup respectively.

12. Arrange the bowls of ranch dressing and ketchup onto the platter over the board.
13. Arrange the shrimp and remaining ingredients onto the platter around the bowls and serve.

Per Serving:
Calories: 652| Fat: 30.3g| Carbs: 60.1g| Fiber: 8.4g| Protein: 36.9g

FISH STICKS BOARD
Prep Time: 25 mins.| Cook Time: 20 mins.| Serves: 6

- 1 lb. tilapia fillets, cut into strips
- 1 C. almond flour
- Salt and ground black pepper, as needed
- 2 large eggs, beaten
- 1½ C. Parmesan cheese, shredded

For Board
- 1 C. guacamole
- 1 C. BBQ sauce
- ¼ lb. bocconcini
- 2 C. cheddar cheese, cubed
- 3 C. potato chips
- 2 C. seeds crackers
- 6 cheddar biscuits
- 3 C. fresh mixed berries

1. Preheat your oven to 450 °F.
2. Line a cookie sheet with baking paper.
3. In a shallow dish, add the flour with salt and pepper and mix until finely blended.
4. In a second shallow dish, place the eggs with a little water and whisk well.
5. In a third shallow dish, place the cheese.
6. Coat the tilapia strips with the flour mixture, then dip into the beaten eggs and, finally, coat with the cheese.
7. Arrange the tilapia strips onto the prepared cookie sheet.
8. Bake for approximately 18-20 minutes.
9. Remove the fish sticks from heat and set aside for approximately 5 minutes.
10. Arrange a large-sized serving platter in the middle of a wooden board. Set aside.
11. In 2 small-sized bowls, place the guacamole and BBQ sauce respectively.
12. Arrange the bowls of guacamole and BBQ sauce onto the platter over the board.
13. Arrange the fish sticks and remaining ingredients onto the platter around the bowls and serve.

Per Serving:
Calories: 936| Fat: 54.5g| Carbs: 67.1g| Fiber: 6.7g| Protein: 48.2g

ONION RINGS & FRIES BOARD
Prep Time: 25 mins.| Cook Time: 25 mins.| Serves: 6

For Zucchini Fries
- 2 zucchinis, cut into 3-inch sticks lengthwise
- Salt, as needed
- 2 eggs
- ½ C. Parmesan cheese, grated
- ½ C. almonds, finely ground
- ½ tsp. Italian seasoning

For Onion Rings
- ½ C. beer
- ½ C. all-purpose flour
- Pinch of salt and ground black pepper
- 2 onions, sliced into rings
- 1-2 C. olive oil

For Board
- 1 C. ketchup
- 1 C. cheese sauce
- 1 C. yogurt sauce
- 2 C. seeds crackers
- 2 C. seedless grapes
- 1 C. figs, sliced
- 2 C. blueberries
- 1 C. olives, pitted
- 1 C. cherry tomatoes
- ¼ C. candied walnuts

1. For zucchini fries: in a large-sized colander, place zucchini sticks and sprinkle with salt. Set aside for approximately 1 hour to drain.
2. Preheat your oven to 425 °F.
3. Line a large-sized cookie sheet with baking paper.
4. Squeeze the zucchini sticks to remove excess liquid.
5. With a paper towel, pat dry the zucchini sticks.
6. In a shallow dish, crack the eggs and beat.
7. In another shallow dish, blend together remaining ingredients.
8. Dip the zucchini sticks in egg and then coat with the cheese mixture evenly.
9. Place the zucchini sticks into the prepared cookie sheet.
10. Bake for approximately 24-25 minutes, flipping once halfway through.
11. Meanwhile, for onion rings: in a medium-sized bowl, add beer, flour, salt and pepper and with a wire whisk, whisk until smooth
12. Dip all onion rings in beer mixture evenly.
13. Heat oil in a large-sized deep wok over a medium-high heat.

14. Add the coated onion rings in 2 batches and fry for approximately 4-5 minutes.
15. Remove the onion rings from oil and place onto a paper towel-lined dish.
16. Arrange a large-sized serving platter in the middle of a wooden board. Set aside.
17. In 3 small-sized bowls, place the ketchup, cheese sauce and yogurt sauce respectively.
18. Arrange the bowls of ketchup, cheese sauce and yogurt sauce onto the platter over the board.
19. Arrange the zucchini fries, onion rings and remaining ingredients onto the platter around the bowls and serve.

Per Serving:
Calories: 951| Fat: 61.5g| Carbs: 82.1g| Fiber: 9.5g| Protein: 19.5g

BEEF BURGERS BOARD
Prep Time: 20 mins.| Cook Time: 8 mins.| Serves: 8

For Burgers
- 2 lb. ground beef
- Salt and ground black pepper, as needed
- 4 tbsp. unsalted butter

For Board
- ½ C. ketchup
- ½ C. mayonnaise
- 8 sharp cheddar cheese slices
- 2 large heads iceberg lettuce, torn into 8 large chunks
- 8 C. fresh baby greens
- 4 heirloom tomatoes, sliced
- 2 small red onions, thinly sliced
- ¾ C. pickled jalapeño peppers
- 2 C. melon, peeled and chopped
- 2 C. fresh blueberries

1. In a medium-sized bowl, add the beef, salt and black pepper and mix until finely blended.
2. Make 8 equal-sized patties from the mixture.
3. Melt the butter in a large-sized non-stick frying pan over a medium heat and cook the patties for approximately 3-4 minutes per side.
4. Remove the patties from frying pan and place onto a paper towel-lined dish.
5. Arrange a large-sized serving platter in the middle of a wooden board. Set aside.
6. In 2 small-sized bowls, place the ketchup and mayonnaise respectively.
7. Arrange the bowls of ketchup and mayonnaise onto the platter over the board.
8. Arrange the patties and remaining ingredients onto the platter around the bowls and serve.

Per Serving:
Calories: 487| Fat: 25.3g| Carbs: 23.5g| Fiber: 3.5g| Protein: 42.2g

VEGETARIAN BURGERS BOARD
Prep Time: 20 mins.| Cook Time: 25 mins.| Serves: 8

For Burgers
- ½ C. walnuts
- 1 carrot, peeled and chopped
- 1 celery stalk, chopped
- 4 scallions, chopped
- 5 garlic cloves, chopped
- 2¼ C. canned black beans, drained
- 2½ C. sweet potato, peeled and grated
- 1 tsp. ground cumin
- 1/3-½ tsp. ground turmeric
- ½ tsp. red pepper flakes
- ¼ tsp. cayenne powder
- Salt and ground black pepper, as needed

For Board
- 1 C. BBQ sauce
- 1 C. basil pesto
- 8 C. fresh baby spinach
- 2 C. grape tomatoes, halved
- 2 C. cucumbers, sliced
- 1 C. olives, pitted
- ¼ C. dried figs
- ¼ C. dried cherries
- ¼ C. candied cashews
- ¼ C. pistachios

1. Preheat your oven to 400 °F.
2. Line a large-sized cookie sheet with baking paper.
3. In a clean food processor, add the walnuts and process until finely ground.
4. Add the carrot, celery, scallion and garlic and process until finely chopped.
5. Transfer the vegetable mixture into a large-sized bowl.
6. In the same food processor, add the beans and process until chopped.
7. Add 1½ C. of the sweet potato and process until mixture becomes chunky.
8. Transfer the bean mixture into the bowl with vegetable mixture.
9. Stir in remaining sweet potato and spices and mix until finely blended.
10. Make 8 equal-sized patties from the mixture.
11. Now, place the patties onto the prepared cookie sheet.
12. Bake for approximately 25 minutes.

13. Arrange a large-sized serving platter in the middle of a wooden board. Set aside.
14. In 2 small-sized bowls, place the BBQ sauce and pesto respectively.
15. Arrange the bowls of BBQ sauce and pesto onto the platter over the board.
16. Arrange the patties and remaining ingredients onto the platter around the bowls and serve.

Per Serving:
Calories: 467| Fat: 11.5g| Carbs: 77g| Fiber: 15g| Protein: 18.5g

GAZPACHO BOARD

Prep Time: 15 mins.| Serves: 6

For Gazpacho
- 3 large avocados, peeled, pitted and chopped
- 1/3 C. fresh cilantro leaves
- 3 C. vegetable broth
- 2 tbsp. fresh lemon juice
- 1 tsp. ground cumin
- ¼ tsp. cayenne powder
- Sea salt, as needed

For Boards
- 1/3 C. whipped cream
- 1/3 C. plain Greek yogurt
- 1/3 C. Parmesan cheese, shredded
- 2 C. croutons
- 1 C. roasted chickpeas
- 1 C. cucumber, chopped
- 1 C. tomato, chopped
- ½ C. onion, chopped
- 1/3 C. fresh cilantro

1. For guacamole: add all the ingredients in a high-powdered blender and process until smooth.
2. Transfer the soup into a large-sized bowl.
3. Cover the bowl and place in the refrigerator to chill for at least 2-3 hours before serving.
4. Arrange a large-sized serving platter in the middle of a wooden board. Set aside.
5. In 3 small-sized bowls, place the whipped cream, yogurt, Parmesan cheese and lemon wedges respectively.
6. Arrange the bowls of gazpacho, whipped cream, yogurt, Parmesan cheese onto the platter over the board.
7. Arrange the remaining ingredients onto the platter around the bowls and serve.

Per Serving:
Calories: 375| Fat: 25.1g| Carbs: 29.8g| Fiber: 9.8g| Protein: 10.5g

SWEET POTATO SOUP BOARD

Prep Time: 20 mins.| Cook Time: 40 mins.| Serves: 8

For Soup
- 3 tbsp. canola oil
- 2 shallots, sliced
- 2 onions, chopped
- 4 garlic cloves, minced
- 2 tsp. paprika
- 6-8 C. sweet potato, peeled and cubed
- Salt and ground black pepper, as needed
- 8 C. vegetable broth

For Board
- ½ C. Parmesan cheese, crumbled
- ½ C. fresh cilantro, chopped
- ¼ C. Serrano peppers, chopped
- 2 lemons, cut into wedges
- 8 grilled cheese flatbreads, halved
- 8 cooked bacon slices, crumbled
- 2 C. fresh blueberries
- 2 C. fresh blackberries

1. heat oil in a large-sized soup pan over a medium heat and sauté shallot and onion for approximately 3-4 minutes.
2. Add garlic and paprika sauté for approximately 1 minute.
3. Add sweet potato, salt, black pepper and broth and bring it to a boil.
4. Now adjust the heat to low and cook for 26-30 minutes.
5. Remove the soup pan from heat and with a hand-held immersion blender, puree until smooth.
6. In a large-sized serving bowl, place the soup.
7. Arrange a large-sized serving platter in the middle of a wooden board. Set aside.
8. In 4 small-sized bowls, place the Parmesan cheese, cilantro, Serrano peppers and lemon wedges respectively.
9. Arrange the bowls of soup, Parmesan cheese, cilantro, Serrano peppers and lemon wedges onto the platter over the board.
10. Arrange the flatbreads, bacon crumbles and berries around the bowls and serve.

Per Serving:
Calories: 820| Fat: 29.8g| Carbs: 95.3g| Fiber: 12.5g| Protein: 40.7g

TOMATO SOUP BOARD

Prep Time: 20 mins.| Cook Time: 45 mins.| Serves: 8

For Soup

- ✓ 3 tbsp. coconut oil
- ✓ 4 carrots, peeled and chopped roughly
- ✓ 2 large white onions, chopped roughly
- ✓ 5-6 garlic cloves, minced
- ✓ 10 large tomatoes, chopped roughly
- ✓ ½ C. fresh basil, chopped
- ✓ 2 tbsp. tomato paste
- ✓ 6 C. vegetable broth
- ✓ ½ C. coconut milk
- ✓ Salt and ground black pepper, as needed

For Board
- ✓ ½ C. sour cream
- ✓ ½ C. Parmesan cheese, shredded
- ✓ ¼ C. fresh basil, chopped
- ✓ ¼ C. jalapeño pepper, chopped
- ✓ 2 C. croutons
- ✓ 1 bag oyster crackers
- ✓ 1 lb. baby carrots
- ✓ ½ C. almonds
- ✓ 2-3 limes, cut into wedges
- ✓ 8 crusty bread slices, toasted and buttered

1. For soup: melt coconut oil in a large-sized saucepan over a medium heat and cook the carrot and onion for approximately 10 minutes, stirring frequently.
2. Add the garlic and cook for 1-2 minutes.
3. Stir in the tomatoes, basil, tomato paste, and broth and bring it to a boil.
4. Now, set the heat to low and simmer for approximately 30 minutes.
5. Stir in the coconut milk, salt, and black pepper and remove from heat.
6. With a hand-held immersion blender, puree the soup until smooth.
7. Arrange a large-sized serving platter in the middle of a wooden board. Set aside.
8. In 4 small-sized bowls, place the sour cream, Parmesan cheese, basil and jalapeño pepper respectively.
9. Transfer the tomato soup into a large-sized serving bowl.
10. Arrange the bowls of soup, sour cream, Parmesan cheese, basil and jalapeño pepper onto the platter over the board.
11. Arrange the remaining ingredients onto the platter around the bowls and serve.

Per Serving:
Calories: 371 | Fat: 16.9g | Carbs: 45.1g | Fiber: 7.1g | Protein: 13.5g

CARROT SOUP BOARD

Prep Time: 20 mins. | Cook Time: 35 mins. | Serves: 8

- ✓ 2 tbsp. canola oil
- ✓ 1 large brown onion, chopped
- ✓ 1 bell pepper, seeded and chopped
- ✓ 4 garlic cloves, minced
- ✓ 1 Serrano pepper, chopped
- ✓ 1 (2-inch) fresh ginger piece, peeled and sliced
- ✓ 8 carrots, peeled and chopped
- ✓ 2 lemongrass stalks
- ✓ 4 C. water
- ✓ 4 C. vegetable broth
- ✓ Salt and ground black pepper, as needed

For Bowl
- ✓ ½ C. plain Greek yogurt
- ✓ ½ C. feta cheese, crumbled
- ✓ ½ C. fig chutney
- ✓ 8 cooked bacon slices, crumbled
- ✓ 4 tbsp. fresh parsley, chopped
- ✓ 4 grilled cheese flatbreads, halved
- ✓ 2 C. croutons
- ✓ 2 C. fish crackers
- ✓ 2 C. seedless green grapes
- ✓ 2 C. fresh mixed berries
- ✓ 2-3 lemons, cut into wedges

1. For soup: heat oil in a large-sized soup pan over a medium heat and cook the onion and bell pepper for approximately 5 minutes.
2. Add the garlic, turmeric and ginger and sauté for approximately 5 minutes.
3. Add carrots and broth and bring to a full rolling boil.
4. Now adjust the heat to low and simmer for approximately 16-20 minutes.
5. Remove the soup pan from heat and with a hand-held immersion blender, puree the soup until smooth.
6. Arrange a large-sized serving platter in the middle of a wooden board. Set aside.
7. In 5 small-sized bowls, place the yogurt, feta cheese, fig chutney, bacon pieces and parsley respectively.
8. Transfer the carrot soup into a large-sized serving bowl.
9. Arrange the bowls of soup, yogurt, feta cheese, fig chutney, bacon pieces and parsley onto the platter over the board.
10. Arrange the remaining ingredients onto the platter around the bowls and serve.

Per Serving:
Calories: 674 | Fat: 23.5g | Carbs: 97.1g | Fiber: 7g | Protein: 19.5g

FRENCH ONION SOUP BOARD

Prep Time: 25 mins.| Cook Time: 20 mins.| Serves: 6

For Soup
- 4 tbsp. unsalted butter
- 3 large onions, thinly sliced
- 2 tbsp. all-purpose flour
- ½ C. white wine
- Salt and ground black pepper, as needed
- 8 fresh thyme sprigs
- 2 C. chicken broth
- 4 C. beef broth

For Bread Slices
- 6 baguette bread slices
- ¾ C. Gruyere cheese, grated

For Board
- 6 prosciutto slices
- 6 salami slices
- 2 crisp apples, cored and sliced
- 2 pears, cored and sliced
- 2 C. seedless grapes
- ¼ C. dried apricots
- ½ C. pecans
- 3 C. sautéed mushrooms
- 2 C. garlic breadsticks
- 2 C. Caesar salad

1. For soup: melt the butter in a large-sized soup pan over a medium-high heat and cook onions for approximately 22-25 minutes, stirring periodically.
2. Add in the flour and cook for 1 minute, stirring continually.
3. Stir in wine, salt and pepper and cook for 2-3 minutes.
4. Add thyme sprigs, chicken and beef broths and bring to a full rolling boil.
5. Now adjust the heat to medium and simmer for approximately 14-15 minutes.
6. Meanwhile, preheat the broiler of your oven to high.
7. Remove the soup pan from heat and discard the thyme sprigs.
8. Place baguette slices onto a large-sized cookie sheet.
9. Then top each bread slice with Gruyere cheese.
10. Broil the bread slices for approximately 1 minute.
11. Arrange a large-sized serving platter in the middle of a wooden board. Set aside.
12. Transfer the carrot soup into a large-sized serving bowl.
13. Arrange the bowl of soup onto the platter over the board.
14. Arrange the baguette slices and remaining ingredients onto the platter around the bowls and serve.

Per Serving:
Calories: 689| Fat: 36.1g| Carbs: 60.1g| Fiber: 7.9g| Protein: 29.5g

DESSERT BOARD RECIPES

ICE CREAM & FRUIT BOARD
Prep Time: 15 mins. | Serves: 8

- 1 C. whipped cream
- 1 C. strawberry sauce
- 1 C. caramel sauce
- 1 C. hot fudge sauce
- 2 C. vanilla ice cream
- 2 C. strawberry ice cream
- 2 C. chocolate ice cream
- 1 C. assorted candies
- 1 C. assorted cookies
- 1 C. mixed nuts
- ½ C. pretzels
- ½ C. mini chocolate chips
- ½ C. Maraschino cherries
- ½ C. fresh strawberries, hulled
- ½ C. fresh blackberries
- ½ C. fresh blueberries
- ½ C. fresh raspberries

1. Arrange a large-sized serving platter in the middle of a wooden board. Set aside.
2. In 4 small-sized bowls, place the whipped cream, strawberry sauce, caramel sauce and fudge sauce respectively.
3. In 3 medium-sized bowls, place the ice creams respectively.
4. Arrange the bowls of ice cream, whipped cream and sauces onto the platter over the board
5. Arrange the remaining ingredients onto the platter around the bowls and serve.

Per Serving:
Calories: 839 | Fat: 41.9g | Carbs: 114.9g | Fiber: 7.8g | Protein: 11g

YOGURT & FRUIT BOARD
Prep Time: 15 mins. | Serves: 6

- 2 C. plain Greek yogurt
- 1 C. strawberry yogurt
- 1 C. vanilla yogurt
- ¼ C. honey
- 2 large bananas, peeled and sliced
- 1 C. seedless grapes, halved
- 1 C. fresh mixed berries
- 1½ C. honey nut Cheerios
- 1 C. cinnamon toast crunch cereal
- ½ C. granola
- 1/3 C. mixed nuts, chopped

1. Arrange a large-sized serving platter in the middle of a wooden board. Set aside.
2. In 4 small-sized bowls, place the yogurt and honey respectively
3. Arrange the bowls of yogurt and honey onto the platter over the board.
4. Arrange the remaining ingredients onto the platter around the bowls and serve.

Per Serving:
Calories: 381 | Fat: 13.1g | Carbs: 68.1g | Fiber: 7.3g | Protein: 17.8g

CANDIES & FRUIT BOARD
Prep Time: 10 mins. | Serves: 10

- 4 oz. M&M candies
- 3 oz. chocolate-coated caramel candies
- 3 oz. mint candies
- 2 oz. red vines candies
- 3 oz. gummy worms
- 2 C. pretzels
- 3 C. kettle corn
- 4 C. seedless grapes

- ✓ 4 C. fresh strawberries, hulled

1. Arrange a large-sized serving platter in the middle of a wooden board. Set aside.
2. Arrange all the ingredients onto the platter over the board and serve.

Per Serving:
Calories: 282| Fat: 3.7g| Carbs: 61.4g | Fiber: 3.3g| Protein: 4.3g

COOKIES & NUTS BOARD
Prep Time: 10 mins.| Serves: 12

- ✓ 12 truffles
- ✓ 12 caramels
- ✓ 6 chocolate chip cookies
- ✓ 6 lemon cookies
- ✓ 6 butter cookies
- ✓ 6 meringue cookies
- ✓ 12 chocolate-covered pretzels
- ✓ 2 oranges, peeled and sectioned
- ✓ 1 C. chocolate-covered cherries
- ✓ 12 fresh strawberries, hulled and sliced
- ✓ 12 dehydrated strawberries
- ✓ ½ C. fresh blueberries
- ✓ ½ C. fresh blackberries
- ✓ ½ C. candied walnuts
- ✓ ½ C. pecans

1. Arrange a large-sized serving platter in the middle of a wooden board. Set aside.
2. Arrange all the ingredients onto the platter over the board and serve.

Per Serving:
Calories: 826| Fat: 42g| Carbs: 101.7g| Fiber: 5g| Protein: 7.8g

COOKIES & JELLY BEANS BOARD
Prep Time: 10 mins.| Serves: 24

- ✓ 14 oz. cookie butter
- ✓ 13 oz. marshmallow fluff
- ✓ 10 oz. hot fudge sauce
- ✓ 2 C. jelly beans
- ✓ 2 C. gummy candies
- ✓ 24 chocolate chip cookies
- ✓ 24 meringue cookies
- ✓ 24 sugar cookies
- ✓ 24 sandwich cookies
- ✓ 14 oz. Pirouette wafers
- ✓ 1 C. sour cherry candies
- ✓ 6 oz. fresh raspberries
- ✓ 6 oz. fresh blueberries

1. Arrange a large-sized serving platter in the middle of a wooden board. Set aside.
2. In 4 small-sized bowls, place the cookie butter, marshmallow fluff and fudge sauce respectively
3. Arrange the bowls of cookie butter, marshmallow fluff and fudge sauce onto the platter over the board.
4. Arrange the remaining ingredients onto the platter around the bowls and serve.

Per Serving:
Calories: 548| Fat: 15.7g| Carbs: 99.2g| Fiber: 3g| Protein: 5.5g

COOKIES & FRUIT BOARD
Prep Time: 15 mins.| Serves: 8

- ✓ 1 C. chocolate sauce
- ✓ 1 C. honey-sweetened yogurt
- ✓ ¼ lb. dark chocolate matcha bark
- ✓ 16 chocolate chip cookies
- ✓ 8 large almond biscotti
- ✓ 8 madeleines
- ✓ 8 caramels, cut into halves
- ✓ 1 C. fresh strawberries
- ✓ 1 C. fresh raspberries
- ✓ 2 blood oranges, peeled and sectioned
- ✓ 1 apple, cored and sliced
- ✓ ½ C. dried cherries
- ✓ ½ C. dried apricots
- ✓ 8 dried persimmons
- ✓ 8 candied dried oranges
- ✓ ¼ C. almonds, toasted
- ✓ ¼ C. walnuts, toasted

1. Arrange a large-sized serving platter in the middle of a wooden board. Set aside.
2. In 2 small-sized bowls, place the chocolate sauce and yogurt respectively
3. Arrange the bowls of chocolate sauce and yogurt onto the platter over the board.
4. Arrange the remaining ingredients onto the platter around the bowls and serve.

Per Serving:
Calories: 682| Fat: 22.6g| Carbs: 110.4g| Fiber: 11.6g| Protein: 10g

POPCORN & TRUFFLES BOARD
Prep Time: 10 mins.| Serves: 8

- ✓ 2 C. chocolate ganache
- ✓ 8 oz. Gouda cheese, cubed
- ✓ 4 C. fresh strawberries, hulled

- ✓ 4 C. caramel popcorn
- ✓ 1 C. pretzels
- ✓ 16 butter cookies
- ✓ 16 truffles

1. Arrange a large-sized serving platter in the middle of a wooden board. Set aside.
2. In a small-sized bowl, place the chocolate ganache.
3. Arrange the bowl of chocolate ganache onto the platter over the board.
4. Arrange the remaining ingredients onto the platter around the bowl serve.

Per Serving:
Calories: 508| Fat: 26.6g| Carbs: 59g| Fiber: 4.8g| Protein: 12.5g

PRATZELS & COOKIES BOARD
Prep Time: 10 mins.| Serves: 12

- ✓ 1 C. Nutella
- ✓ 1 C. vanilla frosting
- ✓ 1 C. fresh blueberries
- ✓ 1 C. seedless red grapes
- ✓ 1 sleeve graham crackers, broken into quarters
- ✓ 1 C. vanilla wafers
- ✓ 1 C. pretzels
- ✓ 1 C. caramel popcorn
- ✓ ½ C. roasted peanuts
- ✓ 12 peanut butter cups

1. Arrange a large-sized serving platter in the middle of a wooden board. Set aside.
2. In 2 small-sized bowls, place the Nutella and vanilla frosting.
3. Arrange the bowls of Nutella and vanilla frosting onto the platter over the board.
4. Arrange the remaining ingredients onto the platter around the bowl serve.

Per Serving:
Calories: 323| Fat: 13g| Carbs: 47.2g| Fiber: 2.5g| Protein: 5.6g

PRETZELS & CANDIES BOARD
Prep Time: 10 mins.| Serves: 20

- ✓ 1½ C. hot fudge sauce
- ✓ 1½ C. honey whipped cream
- ✓ 8 oz. M&Ms candies
- ✓ 5 oz. junior mints
- ✓ 5 oz. milk duds
- ✓ 5 oz. gummy worms
- ✓ 4 oz. red vines candies
- ✓ 6 C. caramel popcorn

- ✓ 2 C. pretzels
- ✓ 3 C. fresh mixed berries

5. Arrange a large-sized serving platter in the middle of a wooden board. Set aside.
6. In 2 small-sized bowls, place the fudge sauce and whipped cream.
7. Arrange the bowls of fudge sauce and whipped cream onto the platter over the board.
8. Arrange the remaining ingredients onto the platter around the bowl serve.

Per Serving:
Calories: 350| Fat: 13.7g| Carbs: 54.7g| Fiber: 3.9g| Protein: 4.7g

CHOCOLATE PRETZELS & WAFERS BOARD
Prep Time: 15 mins.| Serves: 20

- ✓ 16 oz. chocolate pretzels
- ✓ 8 oz. chocolate toffee wafers
- ✓ 14 oz. chocolate hazelnut rolled wafers
- ✓ 11 oz. caramels
- ✓ 7 oz. caramel popcorn
- ✓ 7 oz. Milano cookies
- ✓ 5 oz. chocolate hazelnut cookies
- ✓ 3½ oz. dark chocolate bar
- ✓ 1 lb. fresh strawberries
- ✓ 6 oz. raspberries
- ✓ 6 oz. blueberries
- ✓ 1 C. salted pistachios
- ✓ 8 oz. Brie cheese wheel
- ✓ 1 C. pecans, toasted

1. Arrange a large-sized serving platter in the middle of a wooden board. Set aside.
2. Arrange all the ingredients onto the platter over the board and serve.

Per Serving:
Calories: 600| Fat: 31.7g| Carbs: 71.8g| Fiber: 4g| Protein: 8.2g

CHOCOLATE & DRIED FRUIT BOARD
Prep Time: 10 mins.| Serves: 8

- ✓ 16 chocolate truffles
- ✓ 16 chocolate brownie cookies
- ✓ 4 oz. chocolate-covered candied nuts
- ✓ 2 oz. chocolate bar, chopped
- ✓ 4 oz. almond cookies
- ✓ 4 oz. salted mixed nuts
- ✓ 4 oz. goat cheese, cubed
- ✓ 4 oz. Gouda cheese, sliced

- ✓ 1 large apple, cored and sliced
- ✓ ¼ C. dried apricots
- ✓ ¼ C. dried figs

1. Arrange a large-sized serving platter in the middle of a wooden board. Set aside.
2. Arrange all the ingredients onto the platter over the board and serve.

Per Serving:
Calories: 712| Fat: 45.5g| Carbs: 63.9g| Fiber: 7.2g| Protein: 17.9g

DIPPING SAUCES RECIPES

YOGURT TZATZIKI
Prep Time: 15 mins. | Serves: 12

- 1 large English cucumber, peeled and grated
- Salt, as needed
- 2 C. plain Greek yogurt
- 1 tbsp. fresh lemon juice
- 4 garlic cloves, minced
- 1 tbsp. fresh mint leaves, chopped
- 2 tbsp. fresh dill, chopped
- Pinch of cayenne powder
- Ground black pepper, as needed

1. Arrange a colander in the sink.
2. Place the cucumber into the colander and sprinkle with salt.
3. Let it drain for approximately 10-15 minutes.
4. With your hands, squeeze the cucumber well.
5. Place the cucumber and remaining ingredients in a large-sized bowl and stir to blend.
6. Cover the bowl and place in the refrigerator to chill for at least 4-8 hours before serving.

Per Serving:
Calories: 36 | Fat: 0.6g | Carbs: 4.5g | Fiber: 0.3g | Protein: 2.7g

LEMONY FETA SAUCE
Prep Time: 10 mins. | Serves: 6

- 1 C. feta cheese, drained and crumbled
- 1/3 C. fresh lemon juice
- 1 tbsp. olive oil
- 1 tbsp. fresh mint, finely chopped
- 1 tbsp. fresh dill, finely chopped
- ½ of small Spanish onion, finely chopped
- 1 tbsp. olive oil

1. In a medium-sized bowl, add the feta, lemon juice and olive oil and with a potato masher, mash until smooth.
2. Add the mint and dill and stir to blend.
3. Transfer the sauce into a serving glass bowl and top with onion.
4. Drizzle with olive oil and serve.

Per Serving:
Calories: 113 | Fat: 10.1g | Carbs: 2.2g | Fiber: 0.3g | Protein: 3.9g

WARM CHEESE SAUCE
Prep Time: 10 mins. | Cook Time: 30 mins. | Serves: 8

- Non-stick cooking spray
- 1 (8-oz.) package cream cheese, softened
- 1½ C. feta cheese, crumbled
- ½ C. jarred roasted red peppers, chopped
- 3 tbsp. fresh basil, minced

1. Preheat your oven to 400 °F.
2. Grease a baking dish with cooking spray.
3. In a bowl, add cream cheese, feta cheese, red peppers and basil and whisk until finely blended.
4. Transfer the mixture into the prepared baking dish and with a spoon, smooth the surface.
5. Bake for approximately 26-30 minutes.
6. Remove the baking dish of sauce from oven and set it aside to cool slightly.

Per Serving:
Calories: 176 | Fat: 15.9g | Carbs: 2.6g | Fiber: 0.2g | Protein: 6.3g

LEMONY GARLIC SAUCE
Prep Time: 15 mins. | Serves: 8

- 1 head garlic
- 1 tsp. salt
- 2 tbsp. fresh lemon juice
- 1¾ C. olive oil
- 4-6 tbsp. ice water

1. Peel each garlic clove and then cut them in half.
2. In a small-sized food processor, add the garlic and salt and process until the garlic is minced.
3. Add the lemon juice and process until combined.
4. While the motor is running, add ¼ C. of the oil and process until finely blended.
5. Now add 1 tbsp. of ice water and process until finely blended.

6. Repeat this process of blending until all of ice water and oil are consumed and the sauce becomes smooth.

Per Serving:
Calories: 428| Fat: 47.7g| Carbs: 1.3g| Fiber: 0.1g| Protein: 0.3g

WALNUT & BREAD SAUCE
Prep Time: 15 mins.| Serves: 6

- 4 stale white bread slices, toasted, crusts removed
- ½ C. water
- 1 C. walnuts, shelled
- ½ C. olive oil
- 6 garlic cloves, peeled
- Salt, as needed
- 3 tbsp. fresh lemon juice
- 1 tsp. white vinegar

1. In a small-sized bowl, soak the bread in water for approximately 2 minutes.
2. Lightly squeeze the bread slice to remove excess water.
3. In a clean food processor, add the bread slices and walnuts and process until paste forms.
4. Add the olive oil, salt and garlic and process until finely blended.
5. Transfer the mixture to a bowl with lemon juice and vinegar and stir to blend.
6. The sauce is ready to use.

Per Serving:
Calories: 295| Fat: 29.4g| Carbs: 6.3g| Fiber: 1.7g| Protein: 5.7g

BEET HUMMUS
Prep Time: 15 mins.| Serves: 6

- 15 oz. canned beets, drained
- 2 C. cooked chickpeas
- 1 small garlic clove, peeled
- 3 tbsp. tahini paste
- 1-1½ tbsp. fresh lemon juice
- ½ tsp. ground cumin
- ½ tsp. ground coriander
- ½ tsp. sumac
- Salt, as needed
- 2 ice cubes
- 1-2 tbsp. olive oil
- 2 tbsp. fresh parsley, chopped

1. In a clean food processor, add beets, chickpeas and remaining ingredients except for the olive oil and process until smooth.
2. Add ice cubes and process until finely blended.
3. Transfer the beet hummus into a bowl and drizzle with oil.
4. Garnish with parsley and serve.

Per Serving:
Calories: 194| Fat: 7.5g| Carbs: 27.1g| Fiber: 5.7g| Protein: 6.6g

CARROT HUMMUS
Prep Time: 15 mins.| Cook Time: 30 mins.| Serves: 8

- 3 carrots, peeled and chopped roughly
- 3 tbsp. olive oil, divided
- 1 tsp. paprika, divided
- Salt, as needed
- 1 garlic clove, peeled
- 1 (15-oz.) can chickpeas, rinsed and drained
- 1½ tbsp. tahini
- 2 tbsp. fresh lemon juice
- 6 tbsp. water
- ½ tsp. ground cumin

1. Preheat your oven to 400 °F.
2. Place the carrots, 1 tbsp. of oil, ½ tsp. of paprika and a pinch of salt in a bowl and toss to blend.
3. Then, place the carrot pieces onto a baking sheet.
4. Bake for approximately 25 minutes.
5. Place the garlic clove onto the cookie sheet with carrot pieces and bake for approximately 10 minutes.
6. Remove from the oven and set aside to cool.
7. In a clean food processor, add the carrot, garlic and remaining ingredients and process until finely blended and smooth.
8. Serve immediately.

Per Serving:
Calories: 252| Fat: 8.3g| Carbs: 35.5g| Fiber: 10.2g| Protein: 11g

CHICKPEAS HUMMUS
Prep Time: 15 mins.| Serves: 6

- ¼ C. tahini, well-stirred

- ¼ C. fresh lemon juice
- 1 small garlic clove, minced
- 3 tbsp. olive oil, divided
- ½ tsp. ground cumin
- 1 (15-oz.) can chickpeas, drained
- 2-3 tbsp. water
- Pinch of paprika

1. In a clean food processor, add the tahini and lemon juice and pule for approximately 1 minute.
2. Add the garlic, 2 tbsp. of oil and cumin and process for approximately 30 seconds
3. Scrape the sides and bottom of food processor and process for approximately 30 seconds further.
4. Add half of the chickpeas and process for approximately 1 minute.
5. Add remaining chickpeas and process for approximately 1-2 minutes or until just smooth.
6. Add water and process until smooth.
7. Now, place the hummus into a serving bowl.
8. Top the hummus with remaining oil and paprika and serve.

Per Serving:
Calories: 187| Fat: 13.4g| Carbs: 12.9g| Fiber: 3.1g| Protein: 6g

WHITE BEANS SAUCE
Prep Time: 15 mins.| Serves: 6

- ½ C. olive oil
- 2 tbsp. garlic cloves, chopped
- 2 (16-oz.) cans white beans, drained and rinsed
- 1/3 C. fresh lemon juice
- 4 tbsp. fresh parsley, chopped and divided
- 1 tsp. ground cumin
- ½ tbsp. salt
- 1 tsp. ground white pepper

1. In a small-sized saucepan, place the olive oil and garlic over a medium-low heat and cook for 1½-2 minutes, stirring continually.
2. Remove the pan of garlic oil from heat and set it aside to cool slightly.
3. Strain the garlic oil, reserving both the oil and garlic in separate bowls.
4. Place the beans in a food processor, garlic, lemon juice, 2 tbsp. of parsley and cumin and process until smooth.
5. While motor is running, add the reserved oil and process until light and smooth.
6. Transfer the dip into a bowl with salt and white pepper and stir to blend.
7. Serve with the garnishing of remaining parsley.

Per Serving:

Calories: 263| Fat: 18.1g| Carbs: 20.2g| Fiber: 5.7g| Protein: 7g

BABA GHANOUSH
Prep Time: 20 mins.| Cook Time: 40 mins.| Serves: 6

- 2 lb. Italian eggplants, halved lengthwise
- 2 medium garlic cloves, minced
- 2 tbsp. fresh lemon juice
- ¼ C. tahini
- 1/3 C. olive oil
- 2 tbsp. fresh parsley, chopped plus extra for garnishing
- ¾ tsp. salt
- ¼ tsp. ground cumin
- Pinch of paprika

1. Preheat your oven to 450 °F.
2. Line a large-sized, rimmed cookie sheet with baking paper.
3. Coat the cut sides of each eggplant with a little oil.
4. Arrange the eggplant halves onto in the prepared cookie sheet, halved sides down.
5. Roast for approximately 35-40 minutes or until eggplants are tender.
6. Remove the eggplant from the oven and set aside to cool for approximately 4-5 minutes.
7. With a large-sized scooper, scoop out the flesh from ach eggplant half, leaving the skin behind.
8. Arrange a mesh strainer over a bowl.
9. Place the eggplant flesh into the strainer and discard any stray bits.
10. With your hands, remove the moisture from the eggplant.
11. In a bowl, add the eggplant flesh, garlic and lemon juice and with a fork, mix vigorously.
12. Add the tahini and mix until finely blended. Slowly, add the oil, stirring continually until creamy and smooth.
13. Add 2 tbsp. of the parsley, salt and cumin and mix until finely blended.
14. Transfer the eggplant mixture into a serving bowl and drizzle with a little oil.
15. Top with paprika and parsley serve.

Per Serving:
Calories: 197| Fat: 16.9g| Carbs: 11.6g| Fiber: 6.4g| Protein: 3.4g

PESTO SAUCE
Prep Time: 10 mins.| Serves: 6

- 2 C. fresh basil
- 4 garlic cloves, peeled
- 2/3 C. Parmesan cheese, grated

- 1/3 C. pine nuts
- ½ C. olive oil
- Salt and ground black pepper, as needed

1. Place the basil, garlic, Parmesan cheese and pine nuts in a food processor and process until mixture becomes chunky.
2. Now add the oil slowly and process until smooth.
3. Now, add the salt and pepper and process until finely blended.
4. Serve immediately.

Per Serving:
Calories: 232| Fat: 24.2g| Carbs: 1.9g| Fiber: 0.5g| Protein: 5g

HERB SAUCE
Prep Time: 10 mins. | Serves: 8

- 6 jalapeño peppers, sliced
- 2 garlic cloves, peeled
- Salt, as needed
- 1 C. fresh cilantro leaves
- ½ C. fresh parsley
- ½ tsp. ground coriander
- ½ tsp. ground cumin
- ½ tsp. ground green cardamom
- 1/3 C. olive oil
- 2 tbsp. fresh lemon juice

1. In a food processor, add the jalapeño, garlic and salt and process until chopped roughly.
2. Add the fresh herbs and spices and process until thick paste forms.
3. Transfer the herb paste into a bowl.
4. Add the oil and lemon juice in the bowl of herb paste and stir to blend.
5. The sauce is ready to use.

Per Serving:
Calories: 82| Fat: 8.7g| Carbs: 1.6g| Fiber: 0.7g| Protein: 0.4g

NUTTY ROMESCO SAUCE
Prep Time: 15 mins. | Serves: 10

- 14 oz. canned fire-roasted tomatoes, drained
- 12 oz. jarred roasted red peppers, drained
- 1-2 garlic cloves, chopped
- ¾ C. raw blanched almonds, toasted
- ¼ C. raw blanched hazelnuts, toasted
- ¼ C. fresh parsley, chopped
- ¼ C. olive oil
- 1 tbsp. fresh lemon juice
- 1 tsp. red wine vinegar
- 1 tsp. paprika
- ½-1 tsp. red pepper flakes
- Salt, as needed

1. In a clean food processor, add all ingredients and process until smooth.
2. The sauce is ready to use.

Per Serving:
Calories: 115| Fat: 10g| Carbs: 5.9g| Fiber: 2.1g| Protein: 2.6g

CHEESY RED PEPPER SAUCE
Prep Time: 10 mins. | Serves: 8

- 1 C. feta cheese
- 1 C. ricotta cheese
- ½ C. jarred roasted red peppers, chopped
- 2 garlic cloves, minced
- Salt and ground black pepper, as needed

1. In a clean food processor, add the feta cheese and process until broken into chunks.
2. Add the ricotta cheese, peppers and garlic and process until smooth.

3. Transfer the sauce into a serving bowl and stir in salt and pepper.
4. Cover the bowl and place in the refrigerator for approximately 1 hour before serving.

Per Serving:
Calories: 96| Fat: 6.5g| Carbs: 3.3g| Fiber: 0.2g| Protein: 6.4g

POMEGRANATE BBQ SAUCE
Prep Time: 10 mins.| Cook Time: 20 mins.| Serves: 6

- 16 oz. bottled pomegranate juice
- 2 scallions, chopped
- 2 garlic cloves, minced
- 10 tbsp. ketchup
- 1 tbsp. soy sauce
- 1 tbsp. molasses

1. In a medium-sized saucepan, add the pomegranate juice over a medium heat and bring it to a boil.
2. Cook for 10 minutes.
3. Add in scallion and remaining ingredients and stir to blend.
4. Adjust the heat to low and cook for approximately 3-5 minutes, stirring periodically.
5. Remove the pan of BBQ sauce from heat and set aside to cool before serving.

Per Serving:
Calories: 88| Fat: 0.1g| Carbs: 22g| Fiber: 0.3g| Protein: 0.8g

FRUITY BBQ SAUCE
Prep Time: 15 mins.| Cook Time: 25 mins.| Serves: 10

- ½ of Habanero pepper
- 1 C. mango, peeled, pitted and chopped
- ½ tbsp. fresh ginger, chopped
- 2 tbsp. garlic, chopped
- ½ C. dates, pitted and chopped roughly
- 1 C. tomato sauce
- ¼ C. apple cider vinegar
- 2 tsp. curry powder
- Salt and ground black pepper, as needed

1. Preheat the broiler of your oven to high.
2. Arrange the Habanero pepper half onto a cookie sheet, cut side down and broil for approximately 5-10 minutes.
3. Remove the pepper from broiler and chop it.
4. In a saucepan, add the Habanero pepper and remaining ingredients over a medium-high heat and bring it to a boil, stirring periodically.
5. Now, set the heat to medium and cook for approximately 9-10 minutes, stirring periodically.
6. Remove the pan of BBQ sauce from heat and set aside to cool slightly.
7. In a food processor, add the mango mixture and process until smooth.
8. Set aside to cool before serving.

Per Serving:
Calories: 48| Fat: 0.2g| Carbs: 11.7g| Fiber: 1.6g| Protein: 1g

MANGO SAUCE
Prep Time: 15 mins.| Cook Time: 6 mins.| Serves: 6

- 2 mangoes, peeled, pitted and cut into chunks
- Salt, as needed
- ¼ C. olive oil
- 2 tbsp. paprika
- 2 tsp. cumin seeds
- 1 tbsp. ground turmeric
- 1 tsp. ground fenugreek
- ½ tsp. ground coriander
- ½ tsp. ground black pepper
- 6-8 garlic cloves, minced
- 2 tbsp. brown sugar
- ½-1 C. water

1. In a bowl, add the mango pieces and salt and gently toss to coat well.
2. Transfer the mango pieces into a jar, and set out in the sun for approximately 5 days.
3. Then, drain the mango pieces, reserving the liquid into a bowl.
4. Arrange the mango pieces onto parchment paper and set aside for approximately 3-4 hours.
5. Heat oil in a small-sized saucepan over a medium heat and sauté the spices for approximately 1-2 minutes.
6. Add the garlic and brown sugar and sauté for approximately 2-3 minutes.
7. Add the mango pieces, reserved juices and water and stir to blend.
8. Remove the pan of mango sauce from heat and with a hand-held immersion blender, blend until smooth.
9. Transfer the sauce into a bowl and set aside to cool before serving.

Per Serving:
Calories: 68| Fat: 3.9g| Carbs: 8.9g| Fiber: 1.2g| Protein: 0.7g

FRUITY SAUCE
Prep Time: 15 mins. | Serves: 16

- 2 navel oranges
- 2 apples, peeled, cored and chopped
- 2 (12-oz.) packages fresh cranberries
- 2 C. celery stalks, chopped
- 3 C. white sugar

1. Grate the peel of both oranges in a small-sized bowl. Set aside.
2. Carefully remove the white membrane and seeds of oranges and discard them.
3. Cut each orange into segments.
4. In a food processor, add the oranges, apples, cranberries, celery and sugar and process until chopped coarsely.
5. Transfer the mixture into a large-sized bowl.
6. Add in reserved orange peel and mix until finely blended.
7. Cover and place in the refrigerator to chill for at least 8 hours before serving.

Per Serving:
Calories: 191 | Fat: 0.1g | Carbs: 48.3g | Fiber: 3g | Protein: 0.4g

PEANUT BUTTER SAUCE
Prep Time: 10 mins. | Serves: 6

- 1 C. creamy peanut butter
- 4 tbsp. low-sodium soy sauce
- 2 tbsp. maple syrup
- 4 tbsp. fresh lime juice
- 2 tsp. chile garlic sauce
- ½ C. water

1. In a bowl, place all the sauce ingredients and whisk until finely blended.
2. Serve immediately.

Per Serving:
Calories: 274 | Fat: 21.7g | Carbs: 13.7g | Fiber: 2.6g | Protein: 11.4g

HONEY MUSTARD
Prep Time: 10 mins. | Serves: 8

- ½ C. stone-ground mustard
- ¼ C. rice vinegar
- ¼ C. honey

1. In a small-sized bowl, put all ingredients and whisk until finely blended.
2. Refrigerate before serving.

Per Serving:
Calories: 84 | Fat: 2.8g | Carbs: 12.2g | Fiber: 1.4g | Protein: 2.6g

HONEY CREAM SAUCE
Prep Time: 15 mins. | Serves: 8

- 2 C. cold heavy cream
- 2 tbsp. honey
- 2 tsp. vanilla extract
- 1/8 tsp. sea salt

1. Freeze a glass bowl and beater attachments of a hand mixer for approximately 10 minutes before using.
2. In the chilled glass bowl, place cream, honey, vanilla extract.
3. Set the speed of hand mixer to medium and whisk until slightly fluffier.
4. Now set the speed of mixer to high setting and whisk until stiff peaks form.
5. Refrigerate to chill before serving.

Per Serving:
Calories: 122 | Fat: 11.1g | Carbs: 5.3g | Fiber: 0g | Protein: 0.6g

CREAMY MARSHMALLOW SAUCE
Prep Time: 15 mins. | Serves: 10

- 1 C. cold heavy cream
- 1 (7-oz.) jar marshmallow fluff
- 1 tsp. vanilla extract

1. In a clean glass bowl, add the whipping cream and with a hand mixer, whisk on high speed until soft peaks form.
2. Add the marshmallow fluff and vanilla extract and whisk until finely blended.
3. The sauce is ready to use.

Per Serving:
Calories: 106 | Fat: 4.4g | Carbs: 16.3g | Fiber: 15.9g | Protein: 0.3g

CARAMEL SAUCE
Prep Time: 15 mins. | Serves: 12

- 4 oz. cream cheese, softened
- 3 tbsp. caramel macchiato creamer
- ½ tsp. vanilla extract
- 1 C. cool whip

1. In a clean glass bowl, add the cream cheese and with a hand mixer, mix until smooth.
2. Add the creamer and vanilla extract and whisk until smooth.
3. Stir in the cool whip and place in the refrigerator to chill before serving.

Per Serving:
Calories: 63| Fat: 5.3g| Carbs: 3.5g| Fiber: 0g| Protein: 0.8g

CHOCOLATE SAUCE
Prep Time: 10 mins.| Cook Time: 2½ mins.| Serves: 10

- 4 C. semi-sweet chocolate chips
- 2 C. heavy cream
- Pinch of salt

1. In a large-sized microwave-safe bowl, add the chocolate chips and whipping and microwave on high for approximately 2-2½ minutes or until melted completely, after every 20 seconds.
2. Remove the bowl of chocolate mixture from microwave and stir in salt until smooth.
3. The sauce is ready to use.

Per Serving:
Calories: 442| Fat: 28.8g| Carbs: 40.6g| Fiber: 2.3g| Protein: 5.6g

HOT FUDGE SAUCE
Prep Time: 10 mins.| Cook Time: 5 mins.| Serves: 8

- 14 oz. sweetened condensed milk
- 1 C. semi-sweet chocolate chips
- 2 tbsp. unsalted butter

1. Add condensed milk and chocolate chips into a medium-sized saucepan over a medium-low heat and cook for 3-5 minutes or until chocolate chips are melted, stirring constantly.
2. Remove the saucepan of fudge sauce from heat and immediately stir in butter until blended finely.
3. Serve hot.

Per Serving:
Calories: 345| Fat: 15.2g| Carbs: 47g| Fiber: 0g| Protein: 5.9g

SHOPPING LIST

Poultry, Meat & Seafood:

chicken wings
chicken sausage
ground turkey
ground beef
ground lamb
racks of lamb
ground pork
pork sausage
breakfast sausage
chorizo sausage
ham
prosciutto
salami
mortadella
coppa
soppressata
calabrese
capocollo
bresaola
pepperoni
bacon
cured pork shoulder
smoked salmon
smoked trout
tuna
tilapia
calamari
shrimp

Dairy:

eggs
whole milk
condensed milk
unsalted butter
salted butter
Greek yogurt
strawberry yogurt
honey-sweetened yogurt
vanilla yogurt
yogurt tzatziki
yogurt sauce
cool whip
caramel macchiato creamer
vanilla frosting
feta sauce
sour cream
heavy cream
whipped cream
honey whipped cream
cheese sauce

cream cheese
Parmesan cheese
mozzarella cheese
cottage cheese
Cotija cheese
goat cheese
ricotta cheese
blue cheese
feta cheese
cheddar cheese
Boursin cheese
stilton cheese
Gouda cheese
Brie cheese
Manchego cheese
Iberico cheese
Cabrales cheese
provolone cheese
Pecorino cheese
Asiago cheese
Havarti cheese
string cheese
Gruyere cheese
Queso Chihuahua
bocconcini

Vegetables & Fresh Herbs:

cornichons
dill pickles
pickled vegetables
sun-dried tomatoes
roasted red peppers
microgreens
baby greens
arugula
spinach
radicchio
zucchini
yellow squash
beets
eggplants
olives
bell pepper
green beans
broccoli
artichoke
sweet potato
potato
hashbrowns
mushrooms
celery
carrot

tomato
cucumber
corn
radishes
lettuce
onion
shallots
scallion
lemongrass
ginger
garlic
jalapeño pepper
Serrano pepper
pepperoncini peppers
peppadew peppers
Habanero pepper
green chili
lemon
lime
rosemary
parsley
basil
thyme
dill
chives
sage
cilantro
mint
oregano

Fruit:

strawberries
blueberries
raspberries
blackberries
cranberries
cherries
banana
apple
pear
kiwi
dragon fruit
mango
orange
grapefruit
figs
dates
pomegranate
peach
cantaloupe
watermelon
grapes
avocado

Seasoning & Dried Herbs:

salt
flaky salt
sea salt
kosher salt
celery salt
garlic salt
white pepper
black pepper
red chili powder
cayenne powder
red chili flakes
red pepper flakes
cayenne powder
paprika
garlic powder
onion powder
cinnamon
nutmeg
ginger
coriander
turmeric
cumin
pumpkin pie spice
garam masala powder
curry powder
Italian seasoning
bagel seasoning
lemon-pepper seasoning
Za'atar
sumac
onion flakes
granulated garlic
fenugreek
thyme
basil
oregano

Extra:

almond milk
coconut milk
Non-stick cooking spray
olive oil
canola oil
coconut oil
all-purpose flour
whole-wheat flour
self-rising flour
coconut flour
almond flour
chickpeas flour
baking powder
baking soda
xanthan gum
protein powder
cocoa powder

cinnamon-sugar
white sugar
brown sugar
honey
maple syrup
molasses
stevia
bacon jam
onion jam
quince jam
fig jam
apricot jam
mango jam
strawberry jam
raspberry jelly
strawberry preserves
mango chutney
fig chutney
cranberry sauce
strawberry sauce
orange sauce
Nutella
chocolate ganache
chocolate sauce
fudge sauce
caramel sauce
buffalo sauce
marinara sauce
BBQ sauce
tomato sauce
ketchup
ranch dressing
smoked salmon dip
chicken liver pâté
peanut butter
cookie butter
marshmallow fluff
Dijon mustard
honey mustard
whole-grain mustard
stone-ground mustard
mayonnaise
tahini
salsa
guacamole
Pico de Gallo
pesto
hummus
fish sauce
soy sauce
chile garlic sauce
Italian vinaigrette dressing
balsamic vinaigrette
balsamic glaze
white wine vinegar
red wine vinegar
balsamic vinegar

apple cider vinegar
white vinegar
vanilla extract
almond extract
oats
quinoa
bulgur
chickpeas
black beans
baked beans
white beans
almonds
walnuts
pistachios
cashews
pecans
hazelnuts
pine nuts
peanuts
macadamia nut cheese
pumpkin seeds
sunflower seeds
coconut chips
coconut flakes
shredded coconut
raisins
dried cranberries
dried cherries
dried apples
dried strawberries
dried tangerines
dried oranges
dried peaches
dried apricots
dried figs
dried persimmon
dried dates
crusty bread
Brioche bread
baguette bread
French bread
ciabatta bread
crostini bread
sourdough bread
cinnamon bread
focaccia bread
whole-wheat bread
white bread
sandwich bread
pita breads
flatbreads
Hawaiian rolls
corn tortillas
bagels
croissants
breadsticks
croutons

pita chips
potato chips
cheddar crackers
fish crackers
oyster crackers
pita crackers
salty crackers
artisan crackers
crisp crackers
seeds crackers
graham crackers
fig and olive crisps
cheddar biscuits
oatcake biscuits
buttermilk biscuits
breadcrumbs
vanilla ice cream
strawberry ice cream
chocolate ice cream
butter cookies
assorted cookies
lemon cookies
Milano cookies
wafer cookies
meringue cookies
almond cookies
chocolate chip cookies
chocolate brownie cookies
chocolate hazelnut cookies
sandwich cookies
almond biscotti
Pirouette wafers
chocolate toffee wafers
chocolate hazelnut rolled wafers

assorted candies
gummy candies
M&M candies
caramel candies
mint candies
red vines candies
sour cherry candies
sour gummy worms
jelly beans
junior mints
milk duds
truffles
caramels
madeleines
caramel popcorn
pretzels
chocolate pretzels
peanut butter cups
chocolate chips
chocolate bar
chocolate matcha bark
chocolate-covered candied nuts
Cheerios
crunch cereal
granola
pumpkin puree
Caesar salad
tofu
vegetable stock cube
vegetable broth
chicken broth
champagne
beer

INDEX

A

all-purpose flour, 15, 16, 18, 21, 26, 38, 48, 52, 65
almond biscotti, 54, 67
almond cookies, 55, 67
almond extract, 26, 66
almond flour, 19, 20, 27, 42, 48, 65
almond milk, 16, 26, 28, 29, 44, 65
almonds, 5, 7, 13, 18, 21, 24, 26, 30, 36, 37, 40, 46, 48, 51, 54, 60, 66
apple, 18, 22, 28, 29, 36, 39, 54, 56, 61, 65, 66
apple cider vinegar, 61, 66
apples, 6, 17, 18, 23, 28, 32, 37, 52, 62, 66
apricot jam, 7, 23, 24, 27, 66
apricots, 18, 29, 37, 40, 52, 54, 56, 66
artichoke, 10, 32, 35, 36, 37, 38, 41, 46, 64
artisan crackers, 39, 67
arugula, 13, 14, 19, 41, 64
Asiago cheese, 37, 46, 64
assorted candies, 53, 67
assorted cookies, 53, 67
avocado, 13, 14, 65
avocados, 13, 14, 22, 32, 34, 50

B

baby greens, 10, 16, 20, 25, 27, 43, 45, 46, 49, 64
bacon, 9, 13, 14, 15, 17, 18, 19, 20, 21, 22, 23, 24, 25, 27, 34, 45, 50, 51, 64
bacon jam, 22
bagel seasoning, 14, 65
bagels, 22, 23, 66
baguette bread, 6, 8, 9, 13, 36, 39, 40, 52, 66
baked beans, 34, 66
baking powder, 16, 18, 19, 20, 21, 23, 26, 29, 30, 65
baking soda, 16, 26, 27, 29, 30, 65
balsamic glaze, 13, 66
balsamic vinaigrette, 8, 66
balsamic vinegar, 38, 66
banana, 14, 27, 29, 65
bananas, 13, 17, 21, 23, 26, 28, 29, 53
basil, 5, 6, 8, 10, 20, 33, 38, 42, 43, 44, 47, 49, 51, 57, 59, 60, 65
BBQ sauce, 42, 43, 44, 45, 46, 48, 49, 50, 66
beer, 48, 67
beets, 58, 64
bell pepper, 11, 18, 27, 32, 38, 44, 51, 64
bell peppers, 10, 17, 33, 39, 42, 45, 46, 47
black beans, 49, 66
black pepper, 5, 7, 8, 9, 10, 15, 16, 18, 19, 20, 25, 27, 33, 34, 35, 36, 38, 41, 42, 43, 44, 45, 46, 48, 49, 50, 51, 52, 57, 60, 61, 65

blackberries, 15, 17, 25, 50, 53, 54, 65
blue cheese, 31, 47, 64
blueberries, 13, 15, 17, 20, 21, 23, 25, 28, 29, 39, 48, 49, 50, 53, 54, 55, 65
bocconcini, 35, 37, 48, 64
Boursin cheese, 22, 64
breadcrumbs, 38, 44, 47, 67
breadsticks, 36, 38, 43, 52, 66
breakfast sausage, 18, 19, 25, 33, 64
bresaola, 38, 40, 64
Brie cheese, 22, 25, 31, 37, 39, 40, 45, 55, 64
Brioche bread, 5, 66
broccoli, 64
brown sugar, 5, 18, 24, 61, 66
buffalo sauce, 42, 43, 45, 66
bulgur, 32, 33, 66
butter cookies, 54, 55, 67
buttermilk biscuits, 15, 67

C

Cabrales cheese, 36, 64
Caesar salad, 52, 67
calabrese, 38, 64
calamari, 38, 39, 64
canola oil, 11, 21, 50, 51, 65
cantaloupe, 13, 22, 32, 65
capocollo, 38, 64
caramel candies, 53, 67
caramel macchiato creamer, 62, 64
caramel popcorn, 55, 67
caramel sauce, 53, 66
caramels, 54, 55, 67
carrot, 27, 28, 42, 43, 45, 47, 49, 51, 52, 58, 64
carrots, 31, 33, 42, 43, 44, 51, 58
cashews, 36, 49, 66
cayenne powder, 17, 18, 42, 45, 47, 49, 50, 57, 65
celery, 41, 44, 45, 47, 49, 62, 64, 65
champagne, 10, 67
cheddar biscuits, 48, 67
cheddar cheese, 15, 18, 19, 27, 28, 31, 33, 34, 37, 39, 40, 42, 43, 44, 48, 49, 64
cheddar crackers, 32, 67
Cheerios, 53, 67
cheese sauce, 24, 45, 46, 48, 49, 64
cherries, 5, 25, 49, 53, 54, 65, 66
chicken broth, 52, 67
chicken liver pâté, 40, 66
chicken sausage, 42, 64
chicken wings, 45, 46, 64
chickpeas, 11, 16, 34, 50, 58, 59, 65, 66
chickpeas flour, 11, 65
chile garlic sauce, 62, 66

68

chives, 5, 6, 7, 25, 28, 65
chocolate bar, 39, 55, 67
chocolate brownie cookies, 55, 67
chocolate chip cookies, 54, 67
chocolate chips, 23, 24, 26, 28, 29, 53, 63, 67
chocolate ganache, 54, 55, 66
chocolate hazelnut cookies, 55, 67
chocolate hazelnut rolled wafers, 55, 67
chocolate ice cream, 53, 67
chocolate matcha bark, 54, 67
chocolate pretzels, 55, 67
chocolate sauce, 17, 24, 54, 66
chocolate toffee wafers, 55, 67
chocolate-covered candied nuts, 55, 67
chorizo sausage, 36, 64
ciabatta bread, 6, 41, 66
cilantro, 11, 34, 39, 42, 50, 60, 65
cinnamon, 5, 6, 9, 18, 21, 23, 24, 26, 28, 29, 30, 53, 65, 66
cinnamon bread, 9, 66
cinnamon-sugar, 23, 66
cocoa powder, 23, 29, 65
coconut chips, 29, 66
coconut flakes, 14, 24, 47, 66
coconut flour, 16, 17, 19, 20, 42, 65
coconut milk, 29, 51, 65
coconut oil, 16, 26, 27, 29, 30, 51, 65
condensed milk, 63, 64
cookie butter, 54, 66
cooking spray, 15, 17, 19, 20, 21, 22, 26, 27, 29, 30, 42, 44, 45, 46, 47, 57, 65
cool whip, 26, 62, 63, 64
coppa, 39, 64
coriander, 11, 25, 58, 60, 61, 65
corn, 11, 14, 31, 34, 53, 65, 66
cornichons, 35, 64
Cotija cheese, 14, 34, 64
cottage cheese, 10, 11, 64
cranberries, 5, 6, 11, 37, 62, 65, 66
cranberry sauce, 29, 30, 66
cream cheese, 15, 16, 17, 18, 19, 20, 21, 22, 26, 32, 39, 57, 62, 63, 64
crisp crackers, 37, 67
croissants, 25, 66
crostini bread, 7, 66
croutons, 50, 51, 66
crunch cereal, 53, 67
cucumber, 14, 22, 31, 32, 33, 41, 45, 47, 50, 57, 65
cucumbers, 22, 33, 39, 40, 41, 42, 44, 49
cumin, 24, 25, 34, 44, 49, 50, 58, 59, 60, 61, 65
cured pork shoulder, 38, 64
curry powder, 61, 65

D

dates, 36, 37, 40, 61, 65, 66
Dijon mustard, 9, 36, 41, 66
dill, 7, 36, 39, 40, 41, 57, 64
dill pickles, 36, 39, 41, 64

E

egg, 18, 20, 21, 23, 24, 25, 26, 28, 29, 30, 42, 43, 48
eggplants, 59, 64
eggs, 13, 14, 15, 16, 17, 18, 19, 20, 21, 22, 23, 24, 25, 27, 34, 38, 41, 44, 47, 48, 64

F

fenugreek, 11, 61, 65
feta cheese, 32, 33, 36, 40, 41, 45, 46, 47, 51, 57, 60, 64
feta sauce, 44, 45, 64
fig and olive crisps, 5, 67
fig chutney, 51, 66
fig jam, 5, 14, 15, 17, 31, 32, 37, 39, 40, 66
figs, 5, 18, 23, 31, 35, 36, 37, 42, 45, 47, 48, 49, 56, 65, 66
fish crackers, 31, 40, 44, 51, 67
fish sauce, 42, 66
flatbreads, 50, 51, 66
focaccia bread, 37, 46, 66
French bread, 6, 10, 25, 66
fudge sauce, 53, 54, 55, 66

G

garam masala powder, 11, 65
garlic, 5, 7, 8, 9, 10, 11, 14, 16, 19, 20, 25, 33, 34, 41, 42, 43, 44, 45, 46, 47, 49, 50, 51, 52, 57, 58, 59, 60, 61, 62, 65, 66
garlic powder, 14, 16, 19, 33, 45, 46, 47, 65
ginger, 5, 11, 27, 28, 42, 43, 51, 61, 65
goat cheese, 14, 36, 55, 64
Gouda cheese, 22, 33, 40, 54, 55, 64
graham crackers, 55, 67
granola, 29, 53, 67
grapefruit, 26, 65
grapes, 17, 18, 21, 22, 23, 26, 31, 32, 36, 37, 39, 41, 42, 47, 48, 51, 52, 53, 55, 65
Greek yogurt, 11, 20, 21, 29, 31, 33, 50, 51, 53, 57, 64
green beans, 33, 34, 64
green chili, 24, 65
ground beef, 43, 44, 49, 64
ground lamb, 43, 64
ground pork, 42, 64
ground turkey, 43, 64
Gruyere cheese, 52, 64
guacamole, 31, 34, 48, 50, 66
gummy candies, 54, 67

H

Habanero pepper, 61, 65
ham, 18, 25, 31, 36, 40, 64
hashbrowns, 27, 64
Havarti cheese, 42, 64
Hawaiian rolls, 41, 66
hazelnuts, 36, 60, 66
heavy cream, 17, 62, 63, 64

69

honey, 5, 6, 7, 8, 9, 10, 14, 15, 16, 19, 20, 21, 22, 23, 24, 25, 26, 27, 29, 39, 40, 44, 45, 46, 47, 53, 54, 55, 62, 64, 66
honey mustard, 19, 20, 25, 44, 45, 46, 47, 66
honey-sweetened yogurt, 54, 64
hummus, 16, 31, 32, 33, 40, 58, 59, 66

I

Iberico cheese, 36, 64
Italian seasoning, 48, 65
Italian vinaigrette dressing, 34, 66

J

jalapeño pepper, 51, 65
jalapeño peppers, 9, 34, 36, 41, 46, 49, 60
jelly beans, 54, 67
junior mints, 55, 67

K

ketchup, 39, 44, 46, 47, 48, 49, 61, 66
kiwi, 18, 21, 32, 65

L

lemon, 5, 6, 7, 8, 9, 10, 11, 14, 16, 21, 22, 28, 29, 32, 33, 38, 39, 41, 43, 45, 46, 47, 50, 54, 57, 58, 59, 60, 65, 67
lemon cookies, 54, 67
lemongrass, 42, 51, 65
lemon-pepper seasoning, 16, 65
lemons, 38, 50, 51
lettuce, 34, 38, 41, 44, 49, 65
lime, 41, 42, 62, 65
limes, 51

M

M&M candies, 53, 67
macadamia nut cheese, 31, 66
madeleines, 54, 67
Manchego cheese, 31, 36, 40, 64
mango, 11, 21, 27, 32, 34, 45, 46, 61, 65, 66
mango chutney, 11, 45, 46, 66
mango jam, 27, 66
mangoes, 61
maple syrup, 8, 9, 11, 18, 19, 20, 21, 22, 23, 24, 25, 27, 28, 29, 30, 62, 66
marinara sauce, 38, 39, 44, 66
marshmallow fluff, 54, 62, 66
mayonnaise, 41, 49, 66
meringue cookies, 54, 67
microgreens, 6, 10, 14, 24, 44, 45, 64
Milano cookies, 55, 67
milk duds, 55, 67
mint, 5, 32, 43, 46, 53, 57, 65, 67
mint candies, 53, 67

mixed berries, 15, 17, 19, 23, 24, 27, 29, 40, 44, 48, 51, 53, 55
mixed fruit, 23, 26
mixed nuts, 7, 19, 29, 43, 44, 45, 47, 53, 55
molasses, 61, 66
mortadella, 35, 38, 40, 64
mozzarella cheese, 13, 20, 28, 32, 35, 38, 39, 41, 42, 43, 44, 45, 47, 64
mushrooms, 19, 34, 43, 52, 64

N

Nutella, 17, 55, 66
nutmeg, 5, 16, 21, 23, 28, 46, 65

O

oatcake biscuits, 22, 67
oats, 29, 30, 66
olive oil, 7, 8, 9, 10, 14, 15, 16, 17, 18, 19, 20, 26, 32, 33, 34, 35, 36, 37, 38, 39, 40, 43, 44, 45, 46, 47, 48, 57, 58, 59, 60, 61, 65
olives, 5, 7, 8, 10, 13, 14, 16, 31, 32, 34, 35, 36, 37, 38, 39, 40, 41, 43, 44, 45, 46, 47, 48, 49, 64
onion, 8, 10, 11, 14, 15, 18, 19, 23, 24, 28, 32, 33, 40, 41, 43, 44, 47, 48, 49, 50, 51, 57, 65, 66
onion flakes, 44, 65
onion jam, 15, 23, 28, 66
onion powder, 14, 19, 33, 47, 65
onions, 17, 34, 44, 48, 49, 50, 51, 52
orange, 7, 21, 22, 25, 38, 39, 62, 65, 66
oranges, 5, 14, 18, 21, 26, 28, 31, 45, 47, 54, 62, 66
oregano, 10, 25, 45, 65
oyster crackers, 10, 41, 51, 67

P

paprika, 25, 33, 34, 36, 45, 46, 50, 58, 59, 60, 61, 65
Parmesan cheese, 5, 8, 15, 16, 17, 19, 20, 37, 46, 48, 50, 51, 59, 60, 64
parsley, 5, 8, 9, 32, 35, 37, 38, 39, 41, 43, 47, 51, 58, 59, 60, 65
peach, 22, 65
peaches, 7, 13, 66
peanut butter, 24, 26, 28, 29, 55, 62, 66, 67
peanut butter cups, 55, 67
peanuts, 55, 66
pear, 36, 39, 65
pears, 52
pecans, 11, 18, 31, 37, 44, 52, 54, 55, 66
Pecorino cheese, 35, 64
peppadew peppers, 37, 65
pepperoncini peppers, 34, 35, 38, 65
pepperoni, 34, 37, 64
persimmon, 21, 66
pesto, 14, 16, 42, 49, 50, 66
pickled vegetables, 36, 64
Pico de Gallo, 34, 66

70

pine nuts, 7, 8, 36, 60, 66
Pirouette wafers, 54, 67
pistachios, 5, 6, 24, 29, 37, 49, 55, 66
pita breads, 31, 32, 40, 66
pita crackers, 43, 67
pomegranate, 6, 21, 37, 61, 65
pork sausage, 15, 23, 40, 64
potatoes, 14, 15, 33, 34, 39, 41, 49, 50
pretzels, 53, 54, 55, 67
prosciutto, 9, 13, 23, 35, 37, 38, 39, 40, 43, 52, 64
protein powder, 19, 65
provolone cheese, 34, 35, 37, 46, 64
pumpkin pie spice, 11, 65
pumpkin puree, 11, 67
pumpkin seeds, 6, 11, 66

Q

Queso Chihuahua, 31, 64
quince jam, 36, 66
quinoa, 28, 29, 66

R

racks of lamb, 46, 64
radicchio, 35, 64
radishes, 14, 22, 32, 33, 35, 40, 42, 45, 65
raisins, 27, 66
ranch dressing, 42, 47, 48, 66
raspberries, 15, 17, 21, 22, 28, 53, 54, 55, 65
raspberry jelly, 14, 23, 66
red chili flakes, 7, 8, 9, 14, 65
red chili powder, 11, 24, 65
red pepper flakes, 7, 10, 20, 32, 34, 35, 37, 44, 49, 60, 65
red vines candies, 53, 55, 67
red wine vinegar, 47, 60, 66
ricotta cheese, 19, 20, 21, 38, 40, 60, 64
roasted red peppers, 8, 35, 38, 57, 60, 64
rosemary, 5, 7, 36, 44, 46, 65

S

sage, 8, 11, 65
salami, 13, 14, 22, 23, 25, 31, 35, 37, 38, 39, 40, 52, 64
salsa, 14, 31, 33, 34, 66
salt, 5, 6, 7, 8, 9, 10, 11, 13, 14, 15, 16, 17, 18, 19, 20, 21, 22, 23, 24, 25, 26, 27, 29, 30, 32, 33, 35, 36, 38, 39, 40, 41, 43, 46, 48, 49, 50, 51, 52, 57, 58, 59, 60, 61, 62, 63, 65
Salt, 8, 10, 11, 14, 15, 16, 18, 19, 20, 24, 25, 27, 32, 33, 34, 35, 36, 39, 41, 42, 43, 44, 45, 46, 47, 48, 49, 50, 51, 52, 57, 58, 60, 61
salted butter, 5, 8, 9, 64
salty crackers, 31, 67
sandwich bread, 24, 66
sandwich cookies, 54, 67
scallions, 22, 32, 49, 61
seeds crackers, 48, 67

self-rising flour, 27, 28, 65
Serrano pepper, 51, 65
Serrano peppers, 50
shallots, 9, 50, 65
shredded coconut, 27, 66
shrimp, 41, 47, 48, 64
smoked salmon, 14, 15, 19, 22, 24, 25, 28, 32, 38, 64, 66
smoked salmon dip, 25, 66
smoked trout, 40, 64
soppressata, 35, 40, 64
sour cherry candies, 54, 67
sour cream, 14, 15, 19, 20, 24, 27, 28, 35, 39, 40, 41, 43, 51, 64
sour gummy worms, 67
sourdough bread, 7, 13, 66
soy sauce, 61, 62, 66
spinach, 18, 20, 27, 34, 41, 42, 44, 45, 49, 64
stevia, 19, 28, 29, 66
stilton cheese, 22, 64
stone-ground mustard, 62, 66
strawberries, 6, 13, 15, 18, 20, 21, 22, 25, 29, 39, 53, 54, 55, 65, 66
strawberry ice cream, 53, 67
strawberry jam, 6, 13, 15, 16, 20, 22, 25, 26, 66
strawberry preserves, 17, 26, 28, 66
strawberry sauce, 53, 66
strawberry yogurt, 19, 53, 64
string cheese, 43, 64
sumac, 58, 65
sun-dried tomatoes, 8, 36, 64
sunflower seeds, 28, 66
sweet potato, 49, 64

T

tahini, 39, 58, 59, 66
tangerines, 7, 66
thyme, 5, 6, 10, 25, 44, 52, 65
tilapia, 48, 64
tofu, 17, 18, 67
tomato, 22, 32, 38, 50, 51, 61, 65, 66
tomato sauce, 61, 66
tomatoes, 8, 9, 13, 14, 16, 17, 18, 19, 20, 31, 32, 33, 34, 38, 39, 40, 41, 43, 44, 45, 46, 47, 48, 49, 51, 60
tortillas, 34, 66
truffles, 54, 55, 67
tuna, 34, 64
turmeric, 11, 17, 18, 24, 49, 51, 61, 65

U

unsalted butter, 5, 6, 7, 8, 9, 10, 11, 13, 14, 15, 16, 17, 18, 19, 20, 21, 22, 23, 24, 25, 27, 28, 33, 34, 45, 46, 49, 52, 63, 64

V

vanilla extract, 18, 20, 21, 23, 26, 28, 29, 30, 62, 63, 66

vanilla frosting, 55, 64
vanilla ice cream, 53, 67
vanilla yogurt, 25, 53, 64
vegetable broth, 32, 50, 51, 67
vegetable stock cube, 27, 67

W

wafer cookies, 67
walnuts, 5, 6, 9, 10, 23, 24, 28, 29, 31, 33, 39, 42, 44, 48, 49, 54, 58, 66
watermelon, 21, 32, 65
whipped cream, 17, 20, 22, 23, 24, 50, 53, 55, 64
white beans, 59, 66
white bread, 23, 24, 58, 66
white pepper, 47, 59, 65
white sugar, 16, 17, 21, 23, 29, 62, 66
white vinegar, 58, 66
white wine vinegar, 34, 66
whole milk, 15, 17, 18, 21, 23, 24, 25, 26, 27, 28, 29, 64
whole-grain mustard, 25, 66
whole-wheat bread, 14, 66
whole-wheat flour, 17, 18, 26, 29, 65

X

xanthan gum, 16, 17, 65

Y

yellow squash, 43, 64
yogurt sauce, 42, 44, 46, 47, 48, 49, 64
yogurt tzatziki, 25, 43, 64

Z

Za'atar, 7, 65
zucchini, 19, 43, 48, 49, 64
zucchinis, 19, 48

Made in the USA
Las Vegas, NV
19 December 2023